The Ground Beneath Her Feet: The Archeology of Liberty Island, Statue of Liberty National Monument, New York, New York

OCCASIONAL PUBLICATIONS IN FIELD ARCHEOLOGY
NUMBER 3

The Ground Beneath Her Feet: The Archeology of Liberty Island, Statue of Liberty National Monument, New York, New York

William A. Griswold
Editor

CONTRIBUTORS

William A. Griswold

Tonya Baroody Largy

Lucinda McWeeney

David Perry

Dorothy Richter

Sarah Whitcher

ARCHEOLOGY GROUP
NORTHEAST REGION
NATIONAL PARK SERVICE
U.S. DEPARTMENT OF THE INTERIOR
2003

Contents

LIST OF FIGURES

LIST OF TABLES

Summary

This book has been written to inform the public about the information gathered from the recently completed three-year archeological project on Liberty Island, New York, NY. The first year, or more accurately the first season, of the project was devoted to thorough, but not exhaustive, documentary investigation of the island. During this time, numerous libraries and archives were visited in an attempt to collect as much information as possible about the island's history and prehistory. Excavations were conducted on a prehistoric shell midden during the second year. This shell midden had first been identified in 1985 during the restoration of the statue. Along with the excavation of the shell midden a geophysical survey was conducted on approximately 2/3 of the island. Several non-invasive prospecting techniques were used to identify buried archeological resources on the island including Ground Penetrating Radar (GPR), Electromagnetic Induction (EM) and Magnetometer. The final year of the project was dedicated to ground truthing, or verifying, the results of the geophysical survey.

The data collected from the archaeological investigations on the island, made famous by the erection of Auguste Bertholdi's "Statue of Liberty Enlightening the World," add additional insight concerning the use of the island during its prehistoric and historic past. Until now, the history and prehistory of the island have rested in the shadows of the much more well-known statue. This book attempts to remedy this situation and to communicate the equally interesting prehistory and early history of the island. In keeping with the goals of the National Park Service's mission of public education, this book has been written for a general audience.

While individual goals were established prior to each season, the overall goals for the project were to develop baseline archeological data for the island to assist park managers in decision-making and to update the archeological information available about the island to inform the public. The collection of baseline information is seen as the starting point for later research rather than the ending point for the three-year study.

Acknowledgments

The editor would like to acknowledge several people who were instrumental in the success of this project. The key individual for getting the project started was Diana Pardue, Chief of Museum Services. Her enthusiasm, encouragement, and prompt support were always appreciated. Also among the management at Liberty Island, I would like to thank Diane Dayson, Superintendent, Cynthia Young, Deputy Superintendent (now acting Superintendent), Frank Mills, Deputy Superintendent, Walter Fleming, Deputy Chief of Maintenance and Peter O'Dougherty, Chief, Maintenance Division. Museum staff who aided us in our investigations included Judith Giuriceo, Curator of Exhibits and Media, Geraldine Santoro, Curator of Collections, Stephen Keane, Registrar, Sydney Onikul, Museum Technician, Kathy Garofalo, Museum Technician, Eugene Kuziw, Park Ranger, and Ruby Hopkins, Personnel Officer.

The editor would also like to extend a gesture of thanks to the Building and Utilities crew on Liberty, chief among them Jeff Marrazzo, B&U Foreman, who generously shared their shop with us so that we could store our equipment. We also owe a debt of gratitude to the Park Police who shared their residence with us as a laboratory so that washing, sorting and flotation could be done.

Logistically, working on an island is a trying experience. Unlike working on most sites, if you need something, or forget something, you can not simply go and get it. A round trip boat ride could take as much as two hours. We would like to thank the captains and staff of *Liberty IV* and the Circle Line boats for transportation each day, and for making those special allowances for unscheduled trips.

Finally, I would like to thank those individuals who aided me in excavating the site, processing the artifacts, and cataloging the plethora of materials. Included among these are Jesse Ponz, Priscilla Brendler, Natalie Liberace, and Mary Troy, Ann Chancey, May Faulk, Emily Lindveit, Weston Davies and Frederica Dimmick.

Several of the contributors to this draft report deserve recognition for operating with academic expertise under the constraining government time schedule. I would personally like to thank Dr. Lucinda McWeeney, Dr. David Perry, and Dr. Sarah Whitcher for their contributions to this report. I would also like to thank Dr. Elizabeth Chilton for her help in identifying the prehistoric ceramics. Dr. Gerald Kelso also deserves recognition for his earlier work on the pollen of Liberty Island. Tonya Largy deserves special recognition for her multiple contributions to this book. Her involvement on the 1985, 1999 and 2000 seasons generated consistency for the project. I would also like to thank Sarah Peabody Turnbaugh who did the editing for the technical brief that we published in 2002. Some of the chapters that Sarah did her wordsmithing wonders on have been incorporated in part in the present book. Additionally, I would like to thank Dr. Steven Pendery for his useful comments on this book. Don Marquis, retired Social Studies Department Head at Nashua High School in Nashua, New Hampshire and my wife Robyn Griswold, deserve special thanks for helping me to focus the writing of the text and the organization of the book.

Tonya Largy would like to thank the many scientists that contributed to the faunal analysis over the last 14 years. In the Museum of Comparative Zoology,

Department of Icthyology, Harvard University, Dr. Melanie L. J. Stiassny, Assistant Curator, and Mr. Karsten E. Hartel, Curatorial Associate, assisted with fish identifications. Mr. Peter Burns helped in identification of fish bone from the 1999 excavation. Mr. Jose Rosado, Department of Herpetology, aided the identification of salamander bones in 1999. In the Department of Malacology, David Backus, Curatorial Assistant, identified gastropods from the 1985 excavation, and in 1999, Mr. Adam J. Baldinger, Curatorial Associate, assisted with bivalve identifications. Dr. Raymond Paynter, Department of Ornithology, also offered advice and use of his department's comparative collection. Dr. David C. Parris, Curator, Bureau of Science, New Jersey State Museum, shared unpublished faunal data from the Pennell site in Little Egg Harbor Township, Ocean County, New Jersey. Dr. Thomas Amorosi, Department of Anthropology, Hunter College, graciously examined the pelican bones at my request. I benefited greatly from discussions with Dr. Frank Dirrigl, Jr., University of Connecticut. Dr. Richard H. Meadow, Director of the Zooarchaeology Laboratory, Peabody Museum, Harvard University, offered work and storage space as well as immeasurable support and advice, as always. Finally, I thank Mr. Dick Ping Hsu, retired NPS Northeast Regional Archeologist, for the opportunity both to participate in the 1985 fieldwork and to study that material. I also thank Dr. William A. Griswold, National Park Service Archeologist and Project Manager for the 1999 excavation, for the opportunity to finally assist in the analysis and reporting of both data sets. While acknowledging assistance from those listed, I fully accept responsibility for any errors or omissions in data.

CHAPTER ONE

HOW IT ALL GOT STARTED

William Griswold, Ph.D.

National Park Service, Northeast
Archeology Group

In 1992 the National Park Service began a program to record all of the archeological resources within parks. Known as the SAIP program, which stands for the Systemwide Archeological Inventory Program, it is intended to be a long-term effort to collect basic archeological information on parks within the NPS system. The guidebook written for the program states:

> "The goal is to conduct systematic, scientific research to locate, evaluate, and document archeological resources under NPS stewardship. Whether the purpose is to make resources available for enjoyment by the people or to conserve them unimpaired for future generations, the most fundamental step is to know the resources. Resulting information about the location, characteristics, and significance of archeological resources will enable planners and managers to make better informed, more effective, and less costly decisions about park management, operations, and development."

The SAIP program is part of a much larger Cultural Resource Preservation Program (CRPP). The CRPP, as the name implies, is a program to manage, not only archeological resources, but all cultural resources within the National Park Service including cultural landscapes, structures, museum objects, and ethnographic resources. Both the SAIP and the

CRPP programs have funds attached to them and both are often used to fund archeological work within the NPS. The three years, or more accurately three seasons, worth of work on the island, have been funded from both SAIP and CRPP sources.

Much of the archeological information that had been collected before 1992 at Liberty Island had been the result of compliance-related research. Section 106 of the National Historic Preservation Act (NHPA) mandates that Federal Agencies take into account the effects of their actions on properties within their care that are in, or eligible for, inclusion in the National Register. For archeologists this means that Federal Agencies must assess the impact that any ground-disturbing project may have on the archeological deposits.

For example, let's say that XYZ park is proposing to dig a trench to put in a new telephone line. Part of the park's legal requirements then are to figure out what damage the installation of this utility will have on the archeological resources. In order to do that, archeologists will dig holes along the path of the proposed utility and try to figure out what, if anything, was there and how it will be impacted by the proposed disturbance. Also known as compliance, this type of research often leaves archeologists with a great deal of data on one area of a site and virtually no information on other areas. Before the SAIP program was begun, often what was known about a site was the sum-total of compliance projects. This often resulted in a one-sided presentation of data to the public.

To counter the one-sided presentation of data, the SAIP and CRPP projects began to fund a more systematic collection of data on sites within parks. For a little more than a decade now, these programs have been funding much of the basic archeological data collection in parks. Since all of the projects submitted compete for limited dollars, we were very lucky in obtaining the funds to conduct various stages of research on the island. The Liberty Island project is one of the first sites in the northern part of the Northeast Region to have the full range of archeological information collected on it through the use of the two funding programs. Publications on the results of work on other sites within the northern part of the Northeast Region are expected to follow.

There are several types of studies described in the NPS-28 (the National Park Service's Cultural Resource Management Guidelines) to collect basic archeological information. The first is the Archeological Overview and Assessment (OA). This document, as defined in *NPS-28*, is written to identify and evaluate potential archeological resources through a thorough investigation of the existing records, documents, and reports. The four-part purpose of the OA for Liberty Island, done in 1998, was to: (1) add to the earlier archeological and historical research; (2) identify archeological sites that could be damaged by construction or maintenance projects; (3) synthesize archeological and documentary data about the site; and (4) identify areas for additional research. After several months of research, an OA was completed for Liberty Island in 1998.

Another type of study used to collect basic information within a park is the Site Identification Study (Site ID). The purpose of a site identification study is to gather additional information about a site through fieldwork. The site identification study can take many forms. While it is most often conducted following the Overview and Assessment, the site identification study can involve focused archeological work on a known site, a geophysical survey of a site, or survey work designed to locate additional archeological sites. Other variations are also seen in the site identification study.

We were lucky enough to have all three types of identification studies funded and conducted on Liberty Island. The Site IDs conducted on Liberty Island included an investigation of a prehistoric shell midden, a remote sensing survey of approximately 2/3 of the island, and the excavation of numerous test-pits to verify the remote-sensing results.

In 1999, excavation of the earlier discovered prehistoric site was begun. The excavation of a utility trench in 1985, during restoration of the statue, had sliced through a shell midden. A shell midden is an archeological term used to describe a trash heap made primarily of shell and shell fragments from clams, oyster, scallops, etc. that represents the final stages of food procurement. In other words, it is what remains after you have eaten your seafood meal. Dick Ping Hsu, then Regional Archeologist, recruited several individuals to aid in the examination and documentation of the site. However, only three days were given to the initial investigations. Nevertheless, soil, shell, and pollen samples were collected, and very preliminary analysis was begun. Budgetary constraints limited the amount of fieldwork that was done during the 1985 investigations. Likewise, money was not available for the flotation or pollen analysis to be written up, or for the site report to be prepared.

Funding was obtained to complete the analysis and to document the site more thoroughly. There were four goals for the 1999 project. The first goal was to complete the analysis of the 1985 research on the fauna (animal and fish bones and shells) and flora (plant remains) obtained from flotation. Flotation, as will be discussed in more detail in later chapters, is a process used to separate small bits of plant and animal remains for identification and analysis. The second goal involved limited excavation of additional test pits within the midden. These limited excavations were conducted to recover additional samples needed to complete the faunal and floral analysis. The third goal of the 1999 project was to define the size of the site, so that it could be protected from any further disturbance. Production of a report summarizing all of the 1985 and 1999 research results was the fourth goal. A technical brief, written for scholars, describing the results of both the 1985 and 1999 archeological projects was published for limited distribution in 2002.

Another component of the 1999 investigations involved a remote-sensing survey

2

of the island. The remote sensing investigations used equipment that did not disturb the ground but gave us an idea of what archeological resources might be buried in different areas of the island. The remote sensing investigations were conducted on approximately 8 of the nearly 13 acres of the island; the modern 20th-century landfills which expanded the island were not included in the geophysical component. The equipment used included Ground Penetrating Radar (GPR), Electromagnetic Induction (EM), and a Magnetometer.

The archeological excavations completed during May and June of 2000 were done to verify, or ground-truth, the results of the remote sensing investigations. In our opinion this step was necessary because the remote sensing equipment is not always accurate. In several cases, remote sensing equipment has provided either false positives (identified features and deposits which do not exist) or false negatives (features and deposits which do exist but are not detected by geophysical investigations). Fifty-five 0.5 x 0.5 meter test pits were excavated on Liberty Island, some to investigate anomalies identified by the remote sensing and others to assess areas where anomalies were not noted. The results of these investigations were presented in a 2001 report.

The following chapters will expand upon the various stages of research outlined here and reveal what we have uncovered from the ground surrounding the statue. While written with a scholarly audience in mind, this monograph is intended not only for the scholar, but also for the educated layman, in keeping with the NPS mission of public education. In some cases, I have taken a heavy hand in editing the chapters included in this book. This has been done for several reasons, but most importantly for readability.

Sources and Further Reading

The National Park Service has produced several booklets and manuals, which detail the various archeological programs. These documents, used by NPS archeologists, provide standards for doing federal archeology. The most important of these documents include *NPS-28, Cultural Resources Management Guidelines, Release Number 4* (U.S. Department of the Interior, National Park Service, Washington, D.C. 1994) and the *Systemwide Archeological Inventory Program* (U.S. Department of the Interior, National Park Service, Washington, D.C. 1992). Several web sites are also available to the public for various NPS excavations. These can be found by browsing at the main NPS web site, www.nps.gov

This general-interest book is not the first book to be published on the Liberty Island project. In 2002, we published a scholarly volume on the shell midden excavations. This book, edited by William Griswold, is titled *Archeology of a Prehistoric Shell Midden, Statue of Liberty National Monument, New York* (Archeology Branch, Northeast Region, National Park Service, Department of the Interior 2002). It was distributed to interested scholars and university libraries throughout the region.

CHAPTER TWO

YOU MEAN THE ISLAND HAS BEEN USED FOR THE PAST THOUSAND YEARS?

William Griswold

National Park Service, Northeast
Archeology Group

The geographic location of Liberty Island, formerly Bedloe's Island, greatly affected its use and development. This was true for both the prehistoric, or era before Europeans arrived, and the historic periods. I will attempt to briefly summarize the prehistory and history of Liberty Island in this chapter. Brief summaries are necessary to understand the archeological discoveries that will be discussed later. Because archeological information is generally broad-based, summaries of the prehistoric periods will involve more that the island itself. Archeological information from the Lower Hudson Valley, New York, New England, and even the Northeast will be discussed. With the advent of European settlement, more specific information is available for Liberty Island. The islands' rich and colorful history is also briefly discussed.

THE ENVIRONMENT

Liberty Island is a small 12.7-acre island in New York Harbor. As a remnant of last glacial age, it is composed of sand and small stones deposited as the glaciers retreated. The last glacial advance, during the Wisconsin Glaciation, covered this portion of the harbor with terminal moraines, large hills made of scoured and churned material that mark the furthest advance of the glaciers. These terminal moraines are visible just to the south on Long Island and Staten Island. Presently, Liberty Island is relatively flat due to modern construction and landscape changes. The whole island presently conforms to an NPS landscape design that, with some alterations, began in the 1930s. Mid-18th-century maps, however, give some indication as to what the original island might have looked like prior to modern alterations. These early maps were not, however, drawn to the standards of modern maps, but they do denote high spots, low spots, and buildings. The original natural elevations probably rose no more than 15 to 20 feet above mean sea level.

As an island in New York Harbor, Liberty straddles two different environmental systems. It is near the end of the 350-mile long Hudson River, one of the major waterways into the interior of the country. The Hudson River starts at a small lake in the Adirondacks and is fed by many different tributaries on its southward journey before it flows into the Atlantic Ocean. Liberty Island is part of the Lower Hudson Valley environment, but is practically at the mouth of the Hudson River.

Liberty Island is also a harbor island and, as such, is part of the coastal landscape. Surrounded by relatively shallow waters, Liberty Island and neighboring Ellis Island were very early on known as two of the three "Oyster Islands" in "Oyster Bay"

Figure 2.1 Map showing the location of Liberty Island.

indicating some of the shellfish which could be found there. The third island is now submerged. The mixing of fresh water from the Hudson and the salt water from the Atlantic, creates an estuary in the harbor, an ideal environment for many fish, shellfish, animals and birds.

Liberty Island was not always an island. The glaciers that covered the harbor reached their maximum expansion sometime around 20,000 years ago. According to Kardas and Larrabee, two scholars who wrote an assessment of the geology and paleoenvironment of neighboring Ellis Island, overall sea level dropped some 300 to 400 feet during glaciation. The continental shelf exposed by the glaciers

would have supported a variety of large animals (fauna) and plants (flora). The rate at which the sea level rose varied through time, however, according to Kardas and Larrabee, Ellis and Liberty Islands would have started out as low hills on the mainland. As sea levels gradually rose due to the melting of the glaciers, Liberty and Ellis Islands would have been gradually enveloped in a marsh and only recently (geologically speaking) would Liberty Island have become an island in the true sense of the word.

The entire surface of the island has been redone several times during its history. As a result all of the native plants and animals have long since vanished.

6

Therefore, it is difficult to determine what once might have been there. However, following the retreat of the glaciers, Liberty Island and the lands of the Lower Hudson were covered by stands of various types of hardwood forests that in turn supported a wide variety of large and small forest animals like deer, raccoon, fox, and turkey just to name a few. This area of the continent would have offered numerous resources to people when they first appeared.

THE PREHISTORY

While many visitors journey to Liberty Island, most don't realize that many things happened on the island before the Statue of Liberty was built. Some visitors arrive on the island with the mistaken belief that the island was built for the statue. The following section briefly summarizes the prehistoric periods in the area.

Paleo-Indian Period

The term "Paleo-Indian" denotes the era of the earliest human occupation in the New World (Table 2.1). Both the timing of the migration(s) and the route(s) that the earliest immigrants took are contested issues, especially in light of recent discoveries made in South America. In addition to the migration of people over the Bering Land Bridge during the last glaciation, possible other routes include both the Pacific Rim, via Japan and China, and the North Atlantic. These ancient newcomers quickly spread out over the Western Hemisphere and hunted animals and gathered plants to survive. Fluted

Period	Dates
Paleo-Indian	12,000 BP – 10,000 BP
Early Archaic	10,000 BP – 8,000 BP
Middle Archaic	8,000 BP – 6,000 BP
Late Archaic	6,000 BP – 3,000 BP
Early Woodland	3,000 BP – 2,000 BP
Middle Woodland	2,000 BP- 1,000 BP
Late Woodland	1,000 BP – 400 BP
Contact Period	Post 400 BP

Table 2.1 Prehistoric Periods of the Lower Hudson Valley

projectile points known as Clovis, so named because of the stone flaking technique that left a "flute" on the obverse and reverse sides, are characteristic artifacts from the period. While radiocarbon dates have been obtained for a couple of sites in the Northeast prior to 12,000 years ago, or 12,000 before present (BP) in archeological lingo, most scholars prefer a date of about 12,000 BP for human entry into the northeastern United States.

The environment of the Paleo-Indian period was different than the present environment. Contrary to some earlier portrayals, McWeeney and Kellogg argue that the glaciers had been gone for several thousand years before man first arrived on the scene about 12,000 years ago. When humans first arrived they found a mosaic of forests which supported numerous plants and animals. Liberty Island, as well as other islands in New York Harbor, was still attached to the mainland at this time.

The archeological evidence for the Paleo-Indian Period in southern New York is fragmentary and incomplete. The fact that Paleo-Indian artifacts have been found in the area indicates that Native Americans were in the region, but we don't have a great deal of information like we do for later periods. The rising ocean levels have undoubtedly covered up many sites which are either below sea level or covered up by drowned river valleys. Research into the Paleo-Indian period is however, continuing and the data acquired about the period is becoming much more interdisciplinary, allowing information to be gathered from a variety of sources.

The Archaic Period

The fluted points that characterize the earlier Paleo-Indian period have disappeared by the time the Archaic period begins approximately 10,000 years ago. The Native Americans, however, continued to hunt and gather. Archeologists generally break down the Archaic period further into Early (10,000–8,000 BP), Middle (8,000–6,000 BP), and Late (6,000–3,000 BP) subperiods. As with the Paleo-Indian period, the Early and Middle Archaic are not well known within the region.

Assessments of the Archaic environment by McWeeney and Kellogg show that the climate fluctuated. Forests continued to dominate the landscape of the Northeast and these forests continued to attract various large and small animals. Archeological discoveries suggests that both Paleo-Indian and earlier Archaic economies were mainly based on the hunting and gathering of interior food resources with specialized camps located around inland lakes and river falls. Raw site numbers, in conjunction with artifact numbers, suggest that a more favorable environment in the Northeast supported a much larger population in the Late Archaic. While agriculture and plant domestication was occurring in other parts of the Western Hemisphere, the Northeast did not participate in this transformation at this time.

Hunting and gathering was not limited to the land. Marine resources were also gathered, with shell fish constituting an important archeological resource of the period. Shell middens are the leftovers from harvesting shellfish, and in the case of the Lower Hudson Valley, they are usually made up of oyster shell. That is not to say, however, that oysters are the only shells in the midden. Other types of shell (clam, cohog, etc.) are also found along with a variety of other things like plant remnants and animal bones. These middens vary in time, size, depth, and composition. All of the calcium contained in the shells helps to neutralize the acids in the soils and preserves artifacts and ecofacts. Ecofacts are products of the environment, like seeds and nutshells, that are preserved in the archeological record. Analysis of the shell middens not only offers insight into the eating habits of the Native Americans, but also can add information about where they settled, when they moved, what they did when at the sites, what they traded, and where they got raw materials. For these reasons, shell middens represent a very valuable source of information to archeologists.

The Woodland Period

Dramatic changes in technology, subsistence, and settlements mark the Woodland period (3,000 – 400 BP). The Liberty Island shell midden dates to this time period. In the Northeast, as elsewhere, the widespread use of ceramics has defined the Woodland period. According to Ritchie, the earliest Northeast pottery type, called Vinette I, appeared on Long Island around 3,000 BP. Changes in vessel types, composition, and decoration are now used to separate and classify the divisions within the Woodland period instead of projectile points. Most scholars break down the period into three sub-periods: Early Woodland, 3,000 – 2,000 BP; Middle Woodland, 2,000 - 1,000 BP; and Late Woodland, 1,000 – 400 BP. The bow and arrow appeared during this time and became a very effective hunting weapon. Later in the Woodland period, plants, most notably corn but also beans, squash, and sunflower, were domesticated. Cultivation of crops became increasingly important in people's diets, at least for those in the inland areas. The people in the interior regions of the Northeast became at least semi-settled if not sedentary during this period, and trade flourished.

Neither Vinette-type ceramics nor domesticated plants have been recovered from the Liberty Island site, to date. However, analyses of other material suggests that the Liberty Island shell midden site is representative of coastal sites of this period. The inhabitants of the region around New York Harbor could draw upon terrestrial, oceanic, estuarine, and riverine resources at different times of the year. Perhaps this availability of resources forestalled the development of domesticates that was occurring elsewhere. Without a need, the movement to cultivation and the reliance upon a staple crop simply may not have been necessary in this coastal area.

The Contact Period

While European contact actually happened in the 16th century with Verazzano, it was the Dutch who first settled in the area. The Dutch came to the New World looking for a Northwest passage through the continent, hoping to capitalize on the silks, spices, and other exotics that lay to the east in the Old World. Earlier repeated attempts had failed, but the Dutch used Henry Hudson in 1609 to again attempt to find a passage. While his efforts were ultimately unsuccessful, Hudson did manage to give the Netherlands a place in the New World. With the advent of the Contact period our ability to tell the tale of the past improves.

Many groups of Native Americans inhabited the area through which Hudson traveled. Furs and pelts acquired from the Indians were extraordinarily important items for European markets. In exchange for these furs and pelts the Europeans traded a variety of houseware, hunting and personal adornment items.

THE HISTORY

Several individuals have written detailed summaries of the history of Bedloe's Island, now known as Liberty Island. I am greatly indebted to them for doing the footwork for the research. The following summary is drawn directly from Levine's *History of Bedloe's Island*, Stokes' *The Iconography of Manhattan Island*, Pitkin's "Summary Structural History of

Fort Wood," and Means' "Fort Wood and Bedloe's Island" all of which are cited at the end of the chapter. Readers interested in more detail than this summary provides are encouraged to consult these works.

The Colonial Period — Bedloe's Island, 1609–1794

Governor Nicholls first granted the island known today as Liberty Island to a Captain Needham on December 23, 1667. Needham then sold it to Isaac Bedloo. Isaack Bedloo (a.k.a Isaac, Isaacq Bedloe, Bedlow), a merchant and shipowner, was the first owner of the island when it was under English control. Disappointed with his original homeland's lack of support of the colonists, Bedloo changed allegiances to England after the occupation in 1664. Before that time, however, he had aspired to several Dutch military and governmental appointments.

After Isaack Bedloo's death, the island passed down to his daughter Mary Bedlow Smith. Smith, after acquiring legal interest in the island from her siblings, went through a form of bankruptcy and sold the island to Adolph Philipse and Henry Lane, New York merchants, in 1732.

During Philipse's and Lane's ownership the City commandeered the island as a quarantine station to prevent smallpox from being brought into the

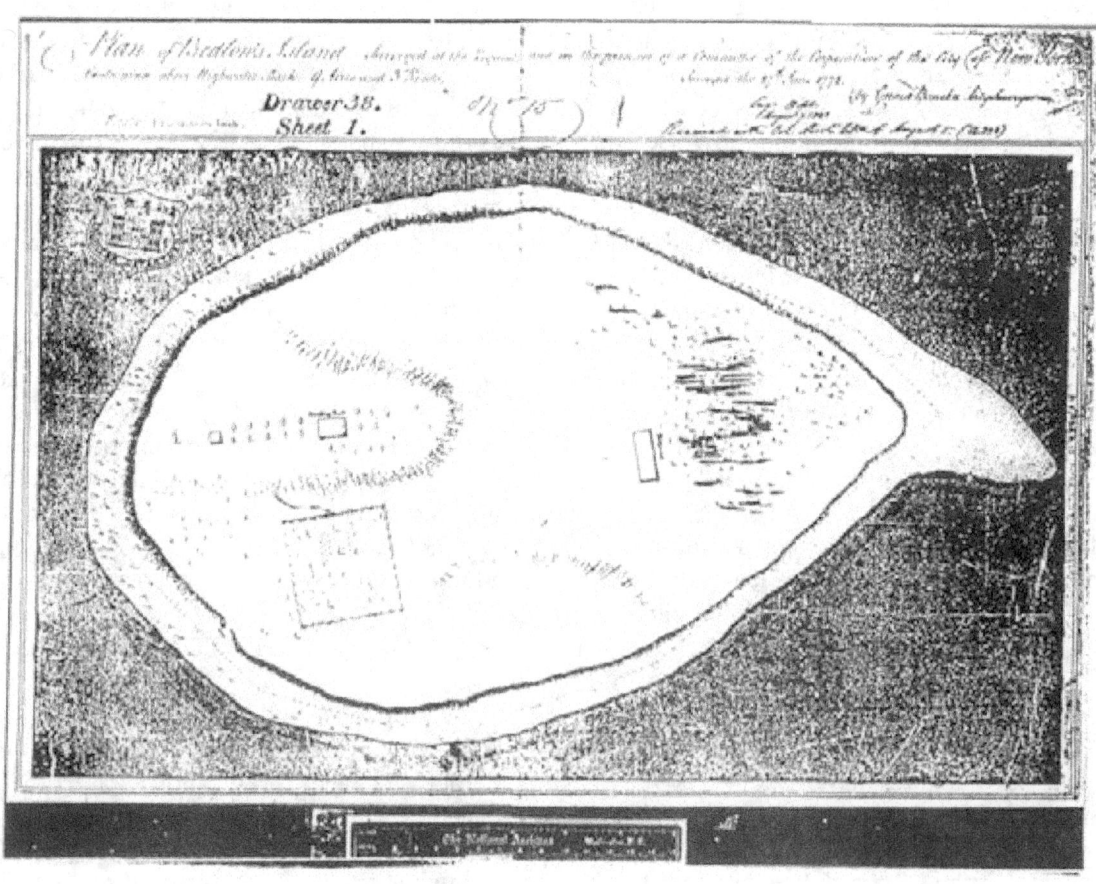

Figure 2.2 1766 Map of the Island (Courtesy of the National Archives)

colony. On January 22, 1746, Archibald Kennedy, Earl of Cassiles, purchased the island. Kennedy was appointed collector and receiver general of the Port of New York, an office that he held more than 40 years, from 1722 to 1763. He is said to have bought the island to use as a summer residence. Kennedy was responsible for recording these early deed transactions.

By 1753 Bedloe's Island had a "Dwelling-House and Light-House" on it and supported a variety of food sources. Beginning around 1756 the island was again used as a quarantine station. Aldermen were later sent from the Corporation of New York to buy Bedloe's Island from Kennedy for not more than 1,000 pounds and to erect upon it a pest house, or quarantine station. The island was finally sold to the city on February 18, 1758, with payments made on June 20, July 20, September 19, and November 13, 1759 for the erection of the pest house.

The island was leased periodically to various tenants for the next few years when not being occupied as a quarantine station. Shortly thereafter, the British used the island to house Tory refugees during the Revolution. As tension between the American colonists and the British mounted the rebels attacked the island, burned the buildings, and made off with the British entrenching tools in April of 1776. Following the Revolution, the Corporation rented the island to various tenants when it was not serving as a quarantine station. The French are noted to have erected buildings here in the 1790s, but no information was found concerning their type or configuration.

The Coastal Defense Period, 1794–1877

After the Revolution, people realized the strategic importance of Bedloe's Island for the defense of New York City Harbor. Situated as it was within New York Harbor, Bedloe's Island provided a clear view of New York City, Governors Island, Ellis Island, and the New Jersey shore. The Corporation of New York opened discussions in 1794 as to whether or not Bedloe's Island should be granted to the State of New York for the purpose of erecting fortifications to defend the city. These negotiations contained a stipulation that when the island was no longer used for fortification it should revert back to the Corporation. Slightly later, in 1796, the French, who had earlier been granted use of the island, were asked to leave. For a while the island then served a dual purpose, part as a fort and part as a pest house. The island was finally delivered to the State of New York on November 2, 1796.

Colonel Jonathan Williams, superintendent of West Point and chief of the U.S. Army Engineers, was appointed in 1807 to survey the defense needs of New York Harbor. Several people realized that the defense system for New York Harbor was inadequate to repel an organized attack. President Thomas Jefferson approved the plan to fortify the harbor that Williams, Vice President George Clinton, and Secretary of War Henry Dearborn proposed, and Williams was instructed to carry it out. In 1814, war-governor Daniel Tompkins named these fortifications Fort Wood in memory of Eleazer Wood, "a distinguished hero in the Battle of Fort Erie".

These constructions survived the War of 1812 without being attacked. However, years of neglect had taken their toll on the constructions by 1820, and the fortifications were described in an Army report to be in ruinous condition. Drawings made in 1839 illustrate that the scarp had suffered substantial deterioration, with some breaches in the fortifications evident. These same illustrations revealed that the fortifications were earthen at the core, faced with masonry.

Beginning in 1844 many changes were made in the fort according to Pitkin. The scarp and main gate were repaired; the

Figure 2.3 Photograph of Fort Wood in 1865.

sallyport was rebuilt; a new magazine, drawbridge, and armaments were added; and the water magazine was greatly expanded. After 1851, Fort Wood also served as a recruiting depot and ordinance depot. In the following 80 years numerous structures developed all over the island.

In 1877 the island was selected as the site for the erection of Auguste Bartholdi's statue of "Liberty Enlightening the World." The Statue of Liberty was a gift from the people of France to the people of the United States in recognition of the centennial of independence and the alliance between France and America during the American Revolution. The monument represented a joint effort by the two nations, with France providing the statue and the United States erecting the pedestal on which it would stand.

A presidential proclamation declared the Statue of Liberty a national monument on October 15, 1924. The War Department, however, continued to administer the remainder of the island. In 1933 the Statue of Liberty National Monument was transferred to the Department of the Interior, National Park Service. Control over the rest of the island was consolidated with that of the statue on September 7, 1937. It was at this time that the entirety of Liberty Island was first

Figure 2.4. Photograph of the island in 1933.

conceptualized as a background for the statue. Norman T. Newton, a National Park Service landscape architect, designed the island's 1937 master plan, which began to be implemented the same year. In subsequent years the island's landscape was transformed, and all of the structures from the Fort Wood period were torn down to implement the landscape design. The buildings present at the northern end of the island are support buildings and residential units dating from the 1940's and 1950's. Several alterations have taken place over the past 65 years of National Park Service ownership, but Newton's overall design concept for the island remains.

As one can see, Liberty Island has a rich history. At some point in time, the island was used by various groups including the Native Americans, Dutch, British,

French, and Americans. It is fortuitous that the island and the statue are, in addition to being one of the crown jewels of the National Park Service, also a World Heritage Site, denoting the site's importance to the world.

Sources and Further Reading

Numerous books, articles, papers and manuscripts were read for the development of this chapter. Most of these are highly scientific, but will provide valuable information to the individual wanting more, detailed information on the selected topics. Most of the information used in this chapter comes from these scholarly works. Susan Kardas and Edward Larrabee's "Report of Archeological

Resources Probability and Significance and Recommendations for Protection, Ferry Slip and Approach Channel, Ellis Island," prepared specifically for the National Park Service in 1976 evaluated Ellis and Liberty Island's paleoenvironment and geological development. This manuscript along with Robert Funk's 1976 *Recent Contributions to Hudson Valley Prehistory*, New York State Museum, Memoir 22 were used to construct the Environment section of this chapter. For the latest paleoenvironmental information readers should see Lucinda McWeeney's and Douglas Kellogg's article "Early and Middle Holocene Climate Changes and Settlement Patterns along the Eastern Coast of North America" in *Archaeology of Eastern North America* 29:187-212 (2001). This article was used for much of the paleoenvironmental information in this chapter. The interested reader is also encouraged to read the entire issue of Discovering Archaeology 2 (2000) which contains several articles on possible migration routes to the New World.

Several books have been written that provide very good summaries of Northeastern prehistory as reflected through archeology. The classic work is William Ritchie's, *The Archaeology of New York State* (Purple Mountain Press, New York reprinted 1994). Ritchie's work provides a detailed regional and chronological development for different groups as expressed through the archeological remains. Another book that provides a more regional perspective on the development of prehistory is *The Archaeological Northeast*, edited by Mary Ann Levine, Kenneth E. Sassaman, and Michael S. Nassanney (Bergin & Garvey: Westport, Connecticut and London 1999). Anne-Marie Cantwell's and Diana diZerega Wall's new book, *Unearthing Gotham: The Archaeology of New York City,* (Yale University Press, New Haven and London 2001) provides a readable account of the prehistoric

development for the New York City area. *Unearthing Gotham* probably provides the best information on what was happening on Liberty Island because of its close proximity to the island. I would be remiss if I didn't mention any of the often groundbreaking works by Dena Dincauze. Dincauze's prolific publications can be found in numerous books and journals. Several important journal articles have also been published that provide a regional perspective on prehistoric development. These include Lucy Lavin's article "Coastal Adaptations in Southern New England and Southern New York," *Archeology of Eastern North America* 16:101-120 (1988), and K. Lightfoot, O Lindauer, and L. Wick's 1984 "Coastal New York Settlement Patterns: A Perspective from Shelter Island," *(Man in the Northeast* 30:59-82 (1984), and H.F. Schaper's "Shell Middens in the Lower Hudson Valley," New York State Archaeological Association *Bulletin* 98: 13-24 (1989). If the reader is interested in reading more concerning the controversy with excavating a shell midden, they should read the different perspectives presented by Dena Dincause and Bruce Borque in the *Review of Archaeology* 17(1) (1998); J. K. Stein's book (ed.), *Deciphering a Shell Midden* (Academic Press, New York et. al., 1992) contains an extensive bibliography on shell middens.

In addition to the regional summaries mentioned above, several scholars have written summaries based on site excavations. Several books are especially important when looking at Liberty Island. These include David Bernstein's *Prehistoric Subsistence on the Southern New England Coast: The Record from Narragansett Bay* (Academic Press, Inc. New York, et.al. 1993), Cheryl Claassen's *Dogan Point: A Shell Matrix Site in the Lower Hudson Valley.* (Occasional Publications in Northeastern Anthropology, No. 14, 1995), and Bruce Borque's *Diversity and Complexity in Prehistoric Maritime Societies: A Gulf of Maine Perspective* (Plenum: New York and London 1995).

Numerous important summary articles have been written about the Contact period and the Native American groups encountered by the Europeans. The classic source for information on these groups comes from the *Handbook of North American Indians, Volume 15, the Northeast* edited by Bruce G. Trigger (Smithsonian Institution: Washington 1978). Chapters by Brasser, Goddard and Salwen are particularly informative for the greater New York City area. H. C. Kraft's 1991 article, *The Archaeology and Ethnohistory of the Lower Hudson Valley and Neighboring Regions: Essays in Honor of Louis A. Brennan*, (Occasional Publications in Northeastern Anthropology No. 11) is also an important source of information.

As mentioned in the chapter, several detailed studies have been done on the history of Liberty Island. Unfortunately, these works are all in manuscript form and are not commercially available. These include G. S. Mean's 1934 "Fort Wood and Bedloe's Island," in *History of the Statue of Liberty*, B. Levine's 1952 "History of Bedloe's Island," unpublished Master's Thesis, New York University, and Thomas Pitkin's 1956 "Summary Structural History of Fort Wood."

CHAPTER THREE

THE EARLY ARCHEOLOGICAL RESEARCH

William Griswold

National Park Service, Northeast
Archeology Group

Prior to the initiation of the current archeological investigations very little archeology had been done at the site. While under NPS control since 1937, only three archeological projects took place on the island. The earliest was conducted by John Cotter, who observed the excavation of the fill between the walls of Fort Wood and the pedestal of the statue in the early 1960s. More than twenty years separated Cotter's work and the next archeological project conducted by Dick Hsu in 1985. Hsu and three other individuals performed only a few days of salvage excavation on a Woodland period shell midden when it was discovered in 1985. Before beginning the current project, I also did work on the island in 1997 for a compliance project. The three test pits excavated for the project observed disturbed deposits and will not be discussed further. This chapter will instead concentrate on Cotter's and Hsu's excavations and what was learned by them.

John Cotter's Excavations (1961-1963)

John Cotter intermittently monitored construction-related excavations at the Statue of Liberty between 1961 and 1963. During this time, the fill that had been dumped between the stone walls of Fort Wood and the base of the pedestal for the statue was removed. This was done for the construction of the American Museum of Immigration (AMI). Since then, the

Museum of Immigration has moved to Ellis Island.

John Cotter took numerous photographs and prepared a short report documenting his work. The photographs in the collection include eighteen color and forty-one black and white pictures of the Manhattan skyline and the construction activities happening on Liberty Island. An unsigned four-page report, presumably written by Cotter was also found which described the who, what, when, why, where, and how of the new construction. Cotter made two trips to the site between November and December of 1961. The goal of the project was written by Cotter on the first page of the report. It was to "to salvage a small collection of artifacts and a minimum of data which would otherwise have been lost" and collecting artifacts and taking photographs of the site. He tried "to relate structures with elements of Fort Wood and the previous quarantine station which occupied the site as referred to in historian Thomas Pitkin's historical report".

The photographs clearly illustrate the dismal conditions under which the artifacts were collected. Large-scale earth moving equipment was brought in to remove the fill deposited between the statue's pedestal and the ramparts of Fort Wood. The photographs clearly show that the bulldozers used for the project were on tracks, compounding the damage done to any archeological deposit. This work was accomplished in just about a month's time.

Figure 3.1 Photograph of the 1960s construction of the AMI.

Large earthen ramps were built over the walls of Fort Wood to remove the fill rather than breaching the fortifications.

Cotter notes the general location of the collected items. Undoubtedly, all he could do was to walk around the area being excavated and look for artifacts and try to identify the general location of the artifacts. He attributed the fill in the pedestal area above the 20-foot level (above sea level) to a mid- to late-nineteenth-century date. Artifacts found within the fill at approximately the 17-foot level, in the vicinity of the old barracks dated to the first half of the nineteenth century according to Cotter. This seems to agree with the historical documents. The artifacts from Cotter's investigations are now stored in the Statue of Liberty/Ellis Island museum.

Dick Hsu's Excavations (1985)

Archeological excavations were done in 1985 on the west side of the main approach to the statue along a utility trench excavated for the restoration of the Statue of Liberty. Dick Hsu, then North Atlantic Regional Archeologist, gathered a small group of people to help investigate a shell midden, located during construction. The project was poorly funded, and the crew spent only three days at the site.

The strategy for the three-day investigation was to collect samples from a pre-midden pit feature, gather artifacts from the feature and the midden, and to sample shells and soil from exposed strata within the midden. Hsu concluded in his report that:

Figure 3.2 Photograph of the 1985 excavations.

The exact extent of the midden could not be determined; along the axis of the trench (north-south) the midden measured approximately 25 meters and east-west at least 5 meters. The thickest portion of the midden, approximately eight meters south of the north end, was approximately 0.5 meter thick. At the north and south margins the midden tapered to less than 10 centimeters thick. Assuming the original configuration of the midden was relatively symmetrical, the western (1/2) portion may still be intact but the eastern (1/3) portion was destroyed when the promenade and walk leading from the landing dock

to the Statue were constructed in the 1940's. Over feature 1, the midden was approximately 15 centimeters thick.

Much of the effort of the 1985 excavations was focused on the examination of a pre-midden pit feature. Hsu comments:

The feature was truncated by the trench; therefore the exact size, shape and orientation couldn't be determined. Projecting from the remnant portion, the total feature was probably 1 to 1.5 meters in diameter at the top and tapered to approximately 0.3 meters at the bottom. Fill in the feature was distinctively darker in profile

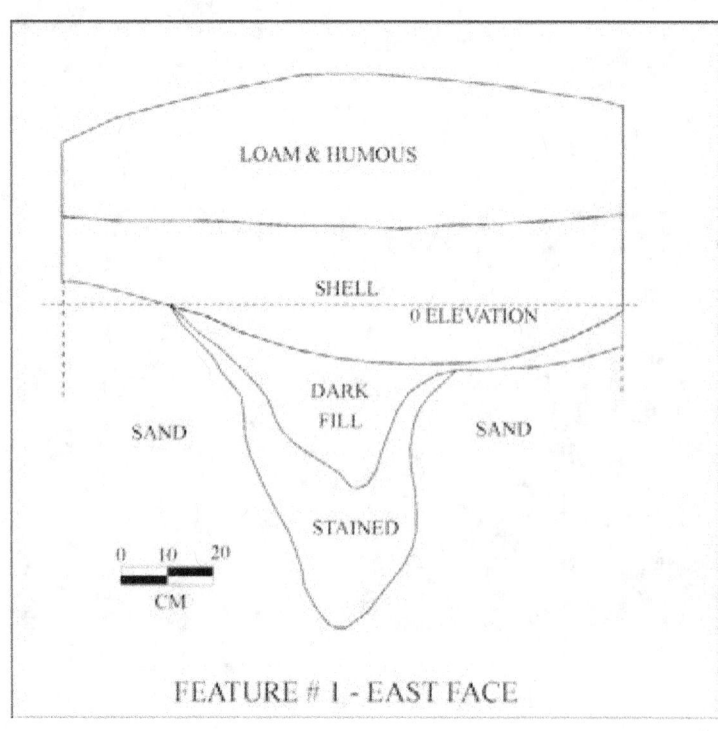

Figure 3.3 Illustration of Feature 1 from the 1985 excavations

20

but less so while excavating. Near the bottom of the pit, several ceramic sherds, bird bones, and fish scales were recovered. Four charcoal samples from four separate areas within the feature were recovered. The shell midden extended over the top of the feature."

Charcoal samples were collected from the feature and were radiocarbon dated. Tonya Largy identified the charcoal from Feature 1 as burned hickory wood and the average radiocarbon date for the samples was about 1000 BP.

Numerous bags of soil were collected from Feature 1 and from the layers of the midden. Afterward, some of the samples were floated in a flotation tank. Flotation is a process used to separate smaller plant and animal remains from the soil. To float a sample of soil, an archeologist will pour the sample into a flotation tank filled with water. The flotation tank contains screens to catch the heavier materials that are not dissolved by the water. This is known as the heavy fraction. While much of the separated material sinks to the bottom and is caught by the screens, some material floats to the top of the water. This material, known as the light fraction, is skimmed off the top. The light fraction usually contains bits of charcoal, carbonized seeds, and other lighter-than-water materials. Both the heavy fraction and the light fraction are sorted and the small plant and animal remains are identified by a specialist. This process allows an archeologist to gather information about layers and features that are typically lost when soils are sifted using the standard ¼" hardware mesh screens. The material recovered by flotation typically passes right through the screens during excavation.

Following the excavations, Tonya Largy analyzed the plant and animal remains that were recovered by the flotation process. However, money was not available for an in-depth examination of the material in

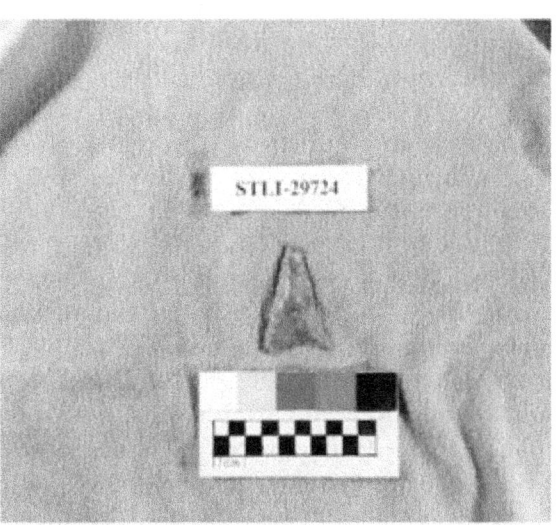

Figure 3.4 Projectile point found during the 1985 excavations.

1985. Tonya had to wait until 1999 to complete the analysis of the flotation samples recovered in 1985.

The lack of archeological investigations at Liberty Island, prior to the current project, is typical for many parks in the region. Some of the parks have had a great deal of research done on them (Minute Man NHP, Colonial NHP), but most have had only a moderate amount of archeology done, at best. The earlier archeological work done on Liberty Island only hinted at the archeological potential of the island.

The following chapters discuss our most recent work on the island. The goal of this work was to try and understand what archeological resources might be left on the island, appraise their research potential, and to figure out how to protect them from future damage. It has taken several seasons of work and hundreds of hours of investigation and analysis to get to our current level of understanding. However, we now believe that we can accurately discuss the remaining archeological resources on the island. The remaining chapters attempt to explain why we believe this.

Sources and Further Reading

Both of the reports discussed in this chapter were prepared by the excavators as short internal memos. They were certainly never intended for commercial publication. While a copy of John Cotter's "Report on Archeological Observations At the American Museum of Immigration Foundation Area, 1962-1963" can be requested from the park, a copy of Dick Hsu's report "Progress Summary Shell Midden Liberty Island, N.Y." can be found in the appendix of William Griswold's (ed.) *Archeology of a Prehistoric Shell Midden, Statue of Liberty National Monument, New York* (Archeology Branch, Northeast Region, National Park Service, 2002).

CHAPTER FOUR

THE HARD SCIENCE BEHIND THE MOST RECENT EXCAVATIONS

Dorothy Richter

Hager-Richter Geoscience, Inc.
Salem, New Hampshire.

Archeological excavation is a destructive process. Once an area has been excavated, it can never be put back together exactly as it was. Believe it or not, the best way to curate artifacts and features is to leave them in the ground. Archeologists have therefore begun to utilize technology from other disciplines to aid them in detecting what may be buried beneath the surface of the ground. This technology, also known as remote sensing, was used on Liberty Island to aid the archeologists in evaluating the possible archeological remains. In many cases, non-invasive remote sensing or geophysical instruments allow geophysicists and archeologists to get a relatively good idea of features and deposits below the ground surface. The results from a geophysical survey are then often used to guide future investigations.

Three different types of geophysical instruments were used to investigate approximately 8 of the 12 acres of Liberty Island. The area of the island that had been created by landfilling operations in the 20th-century was excluded from the survey. Ground Penetrating Radar (GPR), Electromagnetic Induction (EM) and Magnetometry were the chosen for use on the island. Each of these instruments provides different information to the geophysicist of what may lay below the surface. In many cases when used in combination, these instruments provide an accurate reflection of the buried archeological deposits.

METHODS

To conduct the geophysical survey, 8 acres of the island were staked out in 10-meter square units using conventional surveying equipment. To do this, the archeologists used very accurate electronic surveying equipment so that the grid could be re-established over the island when needed. A survey was necessary so that when an anomaly was identified by the geophysicists it could later be located by an archeologist using the grid coordinates. It is similar to laying a sheet of graph paper over a map of the island and marking out an X-Y grid at the intersection of all the lines. When the geophysicists conducted their investigations they further subdivided these 10-meter grids into meter units. All of this was done to accurately control the location of the geophysical investigations so that many of the anomalies could be investigated archeologically.

The initial sweep of the island used all of the instruments and data collection was done at 3 meter intervals. Following the conclusion of the initial sweep, Ground Penetrating Radar (thought to be the most accurate of the geophysical instruments) was used to provide more detailed information on three areas of the island. These three areas of the island then had GPR data collection narrowed down to 1-meter intervals.

Most archeological artifacts do not produce unique geophysical signatures, and the archeological significance of any of the buried features cannot usually be determined on the basis of the geophysical data alone. Sites such as Liberty Island have a long history of occupation and re-working of the landscape, further complicating the interpretation of geophysical results.

Detection and identification must be distinguished. Detection as used in geophysical surveys, is the recognition that an object or feature is present in the ground. Identification refers to determining that the object is a small boulder or a stone implement formerly used to grind grain, a former depression filled with Colonial trash, remnants of a building foundation, etc. Objects of archeological significance do not always have distinctive characteristics that allow them to be distinguished from objects of no archeological significance on the basis of their geophysical signatures. In general, geophysics is an excellent tool for detection of buried features. However, with minor exceptions, if used by itself is poor for the identification and determination of archeological significance of such features.

Ground Penetrating Radar Survey

Ground Penetrating Radar or GPR works by projecting an electromagnetic signal into the ground though an antenna that is dragged across a site. The signal is then deflected by various strata and objects and returns to the surface where it is picked up by a receiver. The reflected signal appears as a profile radar image of the subsurface immediately below the antenna.

Many things affect the GPR signal once it has been projected into the ground. The ability of the soil to conduct and reflect the signal is probably the most important. When the signals return to the receiver and are displayed on a monitor or on paper what the geophysicist is seeing is the differences in travel time as the signal goes through the various strata of soil. If the soils don't contain differences in their conductive properties, the GPR is not going to record a difference in the stratification of the soil. The maximum depth to which GPR signals can penetrate depends on the electrical properties of the soils. Clay minerals and/or brackish water in the ground, for example, pacify the GPR signal, so reflections are not received from materials at greater depths.

The GPR signal penetration at Liberty Island was generally very good, except in the areas of concrete and some local areas with high electrical conductivity. We estimated the potential depth of investigation by the GPR survey was about 3 m below ground surface. However, most of the GPR records show reflections corresponding to 1.5 to 2.3 meters, judged to be an adequate depth for archeological purposes. The GPR signal penetration was generally better on the east side of the island than on the west side of the island.

Electromagnetic Induction Survey

Electromagnetic induction surveys measure the electrical conductivity of the earth. A transmitter causes electrical currents to flow into the ground. Metal objects will distort the electrical currents. A receiver then measures the electrical currents and notes any distortions that have occurred. Buried metal objects, including tools, weapons, household utensils, etc., can then be detected and their locations mapped. One important feature of the EM instruments is that they can detect non-ferrous metal objects that do not show up in a magnetic survey. Metal objects on the surface (manhole covers, metal edging, light posts, etc) will often obscure the signature of metal objects buried beneath them. This is why it is important to use several different detection methods on a site. Geophysicists

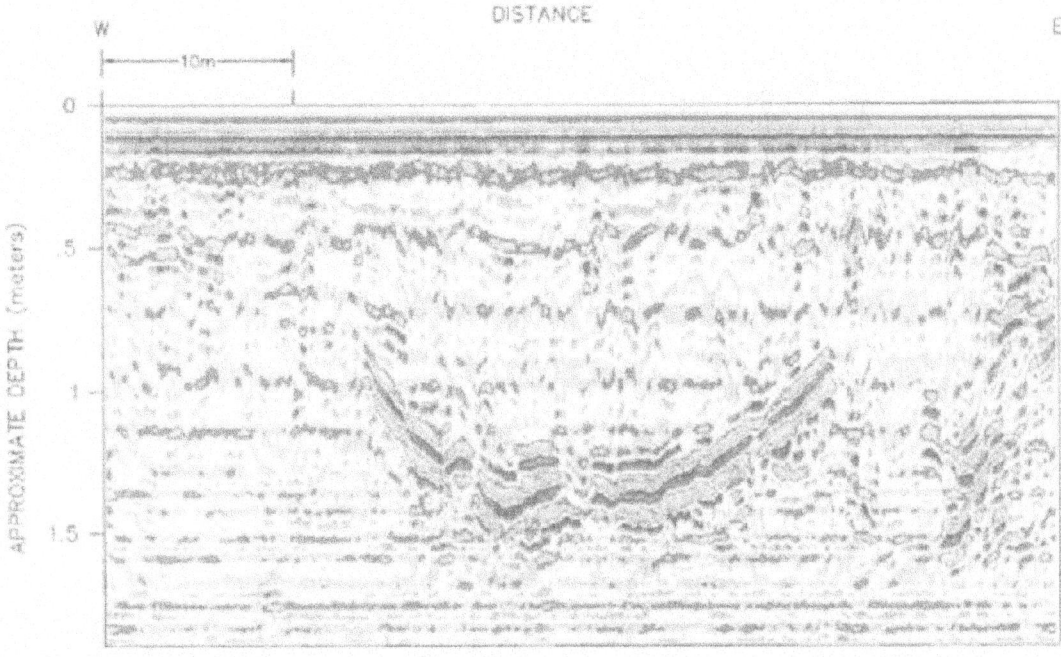

Figure 4.1 Example of a feature detected by GPR.

often use EM surveys to quickly assess large sites so as to identify areas for more detailed investigation with other methods (commonly ground penetrating radar).

The conductivity for most of the survey area on Liberty Island was relatively low, and is typical of sands and soils in the northeastern United States. Most, but not all, of the very high values of apparent conductivity are attributed to observed surface objects, including concrete in extensive areas of the island, air conditioning exhaust vents, metallic edging around trees, and several possible subsurface utilities. Most of the low amplitude anomalies were interpreted to be due to scattered small, metallic subsurface objects.

Magnetic Survey

A magnetometer is used to identify magnetic (i.e. ferrous) objects buried in the earth. Magnetometers can locate most objects containing iron including artifacts containing small amounts of iron, like brick. In this way magnetometers are similar to metal detectors. The magnetometers used by geophysicists are, however, much more sensitive and accurate than traditional metal detectors.

Unfortunately, magnetometers are affected by *all* ferrous objects, even ones above ground. In particular, objects such as dumpsters, small metal buildings, and vehicles, can so influence the magnetic field that buried iron objects can be missed. In areas near above ground ferrous objects, the magnetic data must be supplemented by data from other geophysical instruments to identify buried objects.

Most, but not all of the high values of the total magnetic field and/or magnetic gradient anomalies are attributed to observed surface objects or materials believed to containing iron (reinforced concrete).

25

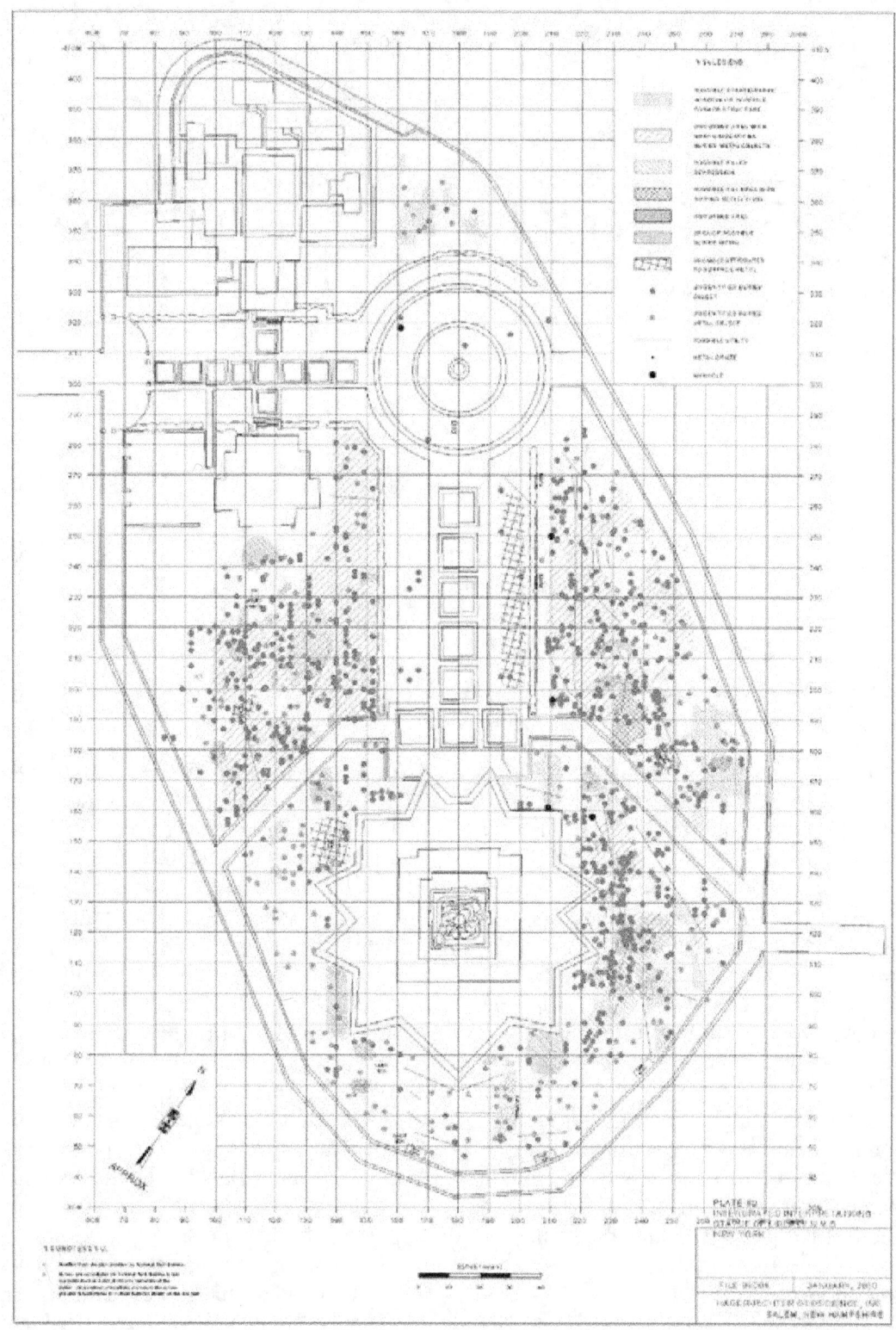

Figure 4.2 Map showing the results of the geophysical survey.

The Integrated Interpretation

The major advantage to using all three techniques (GPR, EM, and magnetometry) is that each instrument provides a separate but complimentary data set. Combining all three data sets provides much more accurate results than using only one geophysical method.

Based on the combined results of the three geophysical methods, many subsurface features were detected and located within the depth of interest for the survey (approximately 1 ½ meters below the ground surface). These include:

- Possible utilities
- Unidentified buried objects (UBO's), some of which are metal
- Flat reflectors due to stratigraphic changes or possibly former structures
- Areas of fill containing small objects
Possible filled depressions
- Disturbed ground and filled former excavations containing UBO's
- Possible sand dune

The shell midden on the west-side of the island did not provide a geophysical "signature" on any of the instruments. A signature would have provided characteristic signs of its existence and aided in the identification of other shell middens on the island. Without a signature, the geophysical team could not provide information on other shell middens that may be on the island.

The data collected from the GPR were examined to see if any of the reflections might correlate with any of the earlier buildings noted in the Overview and Assessment (OA). If you will recall, a large number of earlier maps were discovered during the background research phase of the project. No reflective patterns could be matched to any of the earlier buildings or

building foundations. However, as time and money permit, additional geophysical studies can be done on the island. These studies can fill in the gaps of the wider spaced transects or more intensively explore any of the many anomalies. Although no building foundations were detected, the data recovered through this survey provides archeologists and park managers with a great deal of information about what lies below the ground surface of Liberty Island.

Summary and Further Reading

There are several good introductory journal articles written primarily to educate the archeologist in geophysical methods. While these may be a little technical for the layman, these will provide at least an introduction to the field of archeogeophysics. Recommended articles include: Julia King, Bruce Bevan, and Robert J. Hurry, "The Reliability of Geophysical Surveys at Historic-Period Cemeteries: An Example from the Plains Cemetery, Mechanicsville, Maryland." *Historical Archaeology* 27(3):4-16 (1993) or Jeffrey Wynn "A Review of Geophysical Methods Used in Archaeology," (*Geoarchaeology: An International Journal*, 1 (3): 245-257 (1984). For the more brave at-heart, there is an excellent summary of techniques written for a scholarly audience by John Weymouth, "Geophysical Methods of Archaeological Site Surveying," (*Advances in Archaeological Method and Theory*, Vol. 9, in Michael Schiffer (ed.) pp. 311-395 (1986). There are also a couple of books out on the topic including Lawrence B. Conyers and Dean Goodman, *Ground-Penetrating Radar: An Introduction for Archaeologists,* (Altamira Press, Walnut Creek, London, and New Delhi, 1997) or A. Vogel and G.N. Tsokas, *Geophysical Exploration of Archaeological Sites,* (Braunschweig, Ger., Vieweg 1993).

CHAPTER FIVE

DIGGING INTO MORE THAN DIRT

William Griswold
Tonya Largy
Lucinda McWeeney
David Perry

In 1999 we began excavating in the area where the shell midden had been discovered in 1985. Very little time was devoted to the examination of the midden in 1985. The 1999 excavations were conducted to complete the analysis of the 1985 research, explore additional parts of the midden, define the site boundaries, and produce a report summarizing the research on the shell midden.

METHODS

We used the same grid that had been set up for the geophysical investigations. Although there has been some controversy over how to excavate a shell midden, we chose to use conventional excavation methodology for the small exposure that we did in 1999. Archeology is a destructive process. Once you excavate a test unit, you can never go and put all of the soil back as you found it. It is therefore extremely important that an archeologist records everything that he or she does during the excavation. Everything that was done was recorded on field forms. The field forms provided places for recording information on provenience, soil color and type, artifacts recovered, and the excavator's interpretation for every stratum and every level in all units. The forms also provided a space for the illustration of vertical soil profiles from the sides of the unit as well as plan views (bird's eye views) of the bottoms of the units. Since only two stratigraphic deposits were observed in the 1985 photographs (a stratum of oyster shell, and a dark sand stratum below the shell) this method of separation and recording provided adequate control for the limited amount of exposure done in 1999. All measurements were done in metric.

When excavating, an archeologist tries to peel apart the various layers like one sees in a cake. Normally, an archeologist follows a last in first out methodology, i.e. the latest strata or feature that was deposited is the first taken out. Strata refer to layers, usually horizontal while features refer to manmade construction that usually can't be taken back to the lab. A feature might be a wall, pit, posthole, well, cistern, building foundation, etc. Some strata are thick and at times can represent the accumulation of material over a substantial period of time, sometimes a hundred or more years. Because of this, thick strata were further divided into 10-cm arbitrary levels. In some cases, while a layer may look homogenous, the artifacts in the top level represent a different time period than the artifacts in the bottom level.

All excavation was done by hand, and collected artifacts were bagged and tagged according to their location or provenience. The provenience of an artifact simply means its three dimensional location. In our case the provenience information included the unit coordinate, the stratum or feature that it was collected from, and a depth measurement of the deposit. Artifacts were collected as they were encountered during the excavation. Screening was also done to collect artifacts that may not have been seen by the archeologist during excavation. Screening involves pouring the excavated soil into a box that contains a ¼" hardware mesh screen. The screen is then shaken and the artifacts are picked out and put in the bag containing the materials collected during excavation. These artifacts were then washed on rainy days and brought back to our lab in Lowell, Massachusetts, where they were conserved, cataloged and stored before being returned to the park. In many cases samples of the excavated soils were saved for flotation.

Flotation had previously been done on some of the soil samples retrieved from the 1985 salvage excavations. Most of the 1985 material was floated using a specially designed flotation tank. However, we soon learned that we could obtain better results using simpler equipment. We made this assessment by adding 50 poppy seeds to the samples and counting the number of seeds that were recovered. While the recovery rate was still relatively low, largely because the numerous shell fragments hid many of the seeds, the rate was still higher than that obtained from the traditional flotation tank and the process could be done in a fraction of the time. This streamlined equipment consisted of a new five gallon plastic bucket, two geological sieves (1mm and 2mm), and a fine brine shrimp fishnet.

THE PREHISTORIC MIDDEN DEPOSITS

A total of sixteen 0.5 x 0.5 meter test pits were excavated during the 1999 season of which a portion of the prehistoric shell midden was exposed in four of the units. Three of the four units where the midden was located were opened up into larger 1 x 1 meter units. All of the units excavated contained various layers of historic period materials. The most

commonly recovered artifacts from these layers were brick, coal, and cinder fragments. These artifacts indicate just how pervasive the construction and demolition of buildings was on Liberty Island.

The midden, labeled Feature 9 for the 1999 excavations, varied in thickness from a few centimeters to just over one-half meter. Once the midden was reached two 12" x 12" plastic bags were filled with soil from each level. One 12" x 12" bag of shells was also kept for every level. The shell from the midden was not washed or brushed and neither was any material (except for bone) collected from the prehistoric levels of Feature 9. This should allow future research to be done upon these materials as techniques improve and new types of analysis are introduced.

The soil matrix mixed with the shells was composed of black organic silty sand. Numerous shells were collected from the two and a half meters of exposed deposit. More will be said about the composition of the shell and other fauna obtained from the excavations in later chapters.

While a few small features were discovered below the shell midden stratum, none of these features even approached the importance of Feature 1 discovered in 1985. With the possible exception of Features 11 and 12 (possible a post hole and post mold) the features discovered during the 1999 season could not even be certified as having been constructed, i.e. they may have been the result of natural bioturbation agents. Bioturbation is a word that archeologists use to describe elements like tree roots, small burrowing animals, insects, worms, etc., which move things around in the ground. The excavation of Feature 9 revealed only a handful of artifacts. A few ceramic fragments were uncovered as were a few lithic fragments. A Levanna point uncovered during the 1985 excavation was the only projectile point uncovered from an archeological context.

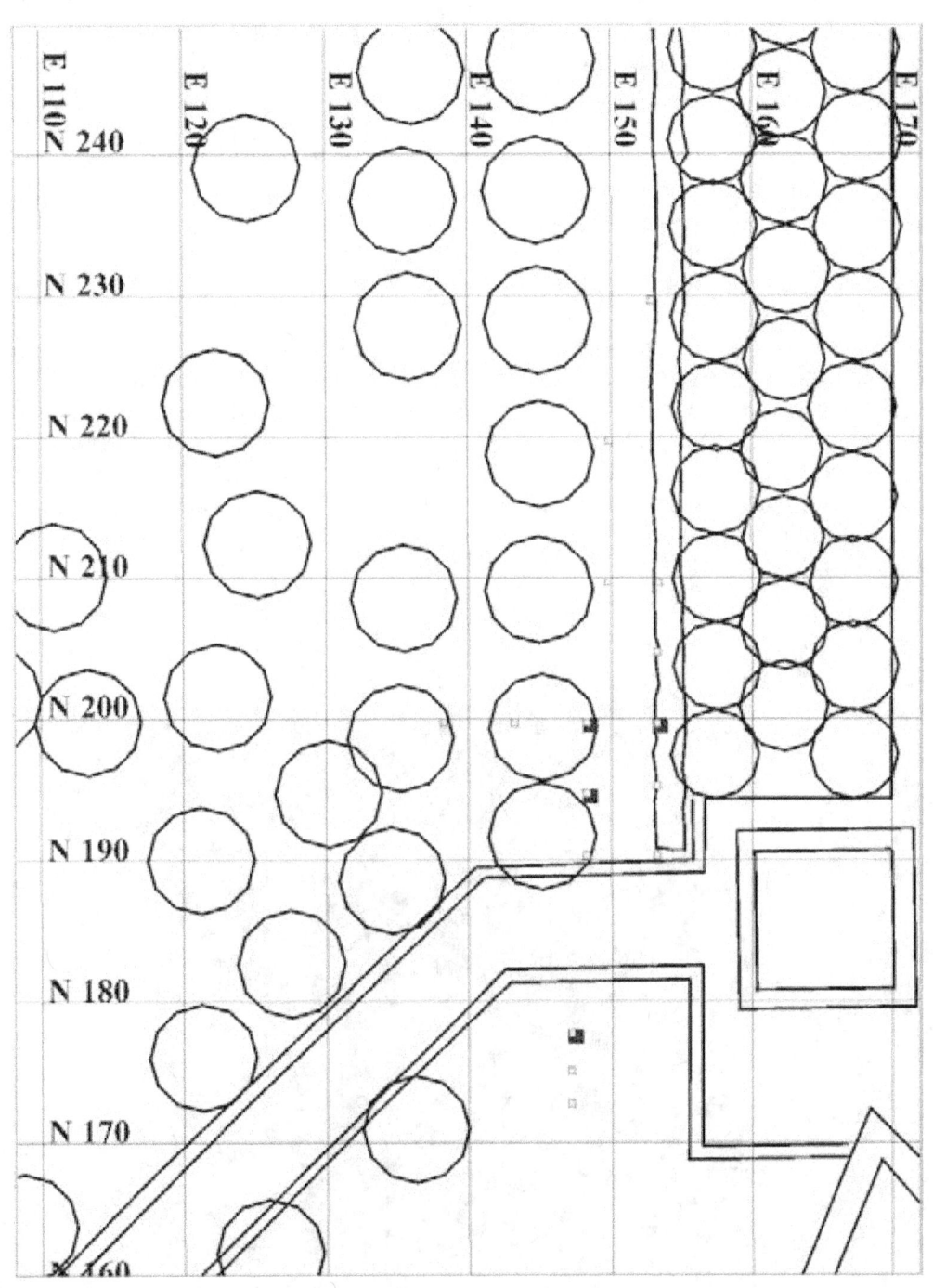

Figure 5.1 Map showing the location of the units tested.

Overall, the 1999 excavations defined the extent of the remaining shell midden. The midden is restricted to an area of approximately 20 meters long (N-S) x 15 meters wide (E-W), or 300 square meters in area. This measurement denotes the maximum lateral extent of the midden if it were square. Most likely, the midden is not square and additional excavations may be able to more tightly define its boundaries. Realistically, the midden is probably no more than 200 square meters in area, but a safety margin has been added to protect the midden from any future construction-related disturbance. It is hazardous to speculate on its original size, but much of the midden was cut away during earlier construction activities at the site. However, now that we know about the midden including its size

and importance for illuminating the prehistory of the area, it can be protected from any future disturbance.

THE RESULTS – FILLING OUT THE PREHISTORIC PICTURE

In order to discover information about the diet and ecology of the Native Americans who used Liberty Island, a detailed analysis of the flotation fractions were undertaken. This type of analysis requires the work of specialists who know, and have worked with, the plants and animals of the Northeast. Many of these specialists have spent years acquiring the background knowledge necessary to undertake these types of analyses.

Figure 5.2 Photograph of the midden as exposed in 1999.

Flora

by Lucinda McWeeney, David Perry, and Tonya Largy

The interpretation of archeological plant remains recovered by flotation is not an easy task, especially in the case of wild plant foods. Before people began to cultivate plants, they relied heavily on wild plants for food. Carbonized seeds from fruits and berries and carbonized nutshell are the most common plant remains preserved in the archeological record. These materials are usually preserved by accidentally falling into a fire during food preparation or by deliberately being discarded and charred in the food processing cycle. However, these same items can also be carbonized by blowing into a fire or by being caught in a generalized "burn" over an area. Sometimes these fires are the result of man and sometimes they are the result of natural events, like a forest fire. Archeologists try to look at the context of the finds to determine whether the seed or nutshell is a result of cultural or natural events.

Wood Charcoal

The identification of charred wood from archeological sites requires the use of low- and high-power reflected light microscopes. Before identification can take place, thin sections are snapped and mounted on glass slides. Thin sections, as the name implies, are very thin slices of the material being examined. The charred wood samples observed under the microscope are then compared to images of previously identified materials available in reference manuals. This allows the researcher to identify the genus and sometimes the specie of the sample.

Trees identified from the 1985 samples included hickory, oak, and conifer. Some other deciduous trees were observed, but could not be identified to the species

level. The presence of hickory was to be expected, since larger burned fragments of hickory wood were submitted for radiocarbon analysis.

The analysis of the wood from the 1999 samples showed oak to be the most dominant wood with lesser amounts of elm and juniper. Oak wood is well recognized for providing a steady, hot fire. The acorn production from trees suggested by the presence of the oak charcoal would certainly have provided a food resource for the people and the animals they hunted.

Seeds and Nuts

Seeds and nut remains are usually recovered from archeological deposits the same way as wood charcoal, namely through flotation. Most of the seeds and nuts are then examined under a microscope to make a positive identification. As with wood charcoal, the images observed with the microscope are compared to standard references for identification.

No charred seeds or pits were found in either the 1985 or the 1999 Liberty Island samples. Some uncharred seeds were identified. These are thought to have been introduced through bioturbation because acids in the soil work to decompose uncharred plant material.

Nutshell, specifically hickory nutshell, was found in abundance. This may be due to preservation factors and may not signal its importance in the diet. In other words, charred hickory nutshell is very hard and preserves well in the archeological record, something that not all other nutshell does. Except for the charred hickory nutshell, the seed/fruit remains from the Liberty Island midden site do not indicate the intensive collection of any single botanical resource. A concentration of hickory nutshell in the shell layer from the 1985 excavations may indicate that nuts may have been gathered contemporaneously with the shellfish. A late summer/fall season of gathering may be inferred from the concentration of nutshell.

Parenchymatous Tissues

The identification of soft plant tissues was also done on the Liberty Island samples. Soft tissues make up most plants with the exception of wood from trees, and seeds or fruits. That is, vegetative tissues include the leaves, stems, twigs, roots, and storage organs of plants. Most of the plant vanishes when the plant dies. However, if the plant is burned, some small charred parts may survive and can be identified. Parenchymatous tissue analysis, or soft plant tissue identification, is a process that allows archeologists to look at a class of material which is only now coming to the forefront of archeological research.

The size of fragments selected can vary greatly. Sometimes only a very small fragment is needed. Fragments less than 2mm in size are difficult to slice and therefore difficult to identify. For this reason, fragments larger than 2 mm were selected for analysis. Once promising fragments had been isolated, they were mounted on a standard metal stub used for analysis under a Scanning Electron Microscope (SEM). The images observed under the SEM are then compared to known images and identifications are made.

Five fragments of probable parenchymatous tissues were isolated from one of the botanical samples taken at the Liberty Island midden. Parenchymatous tissue was seen in many of the samples, but only these five were examined under SEM. Examples of water-lily and flowering rush were identified from the five fragments.

The floral analysis obtained from the 1985 and 1999 flotation samples generated a rich assortment of plants and trees important to the Native Americans during the Woodland and possibly Contact periods. The analysis of the faunal assemblage also indicates that a diverse set of animals and fish were being exploited.

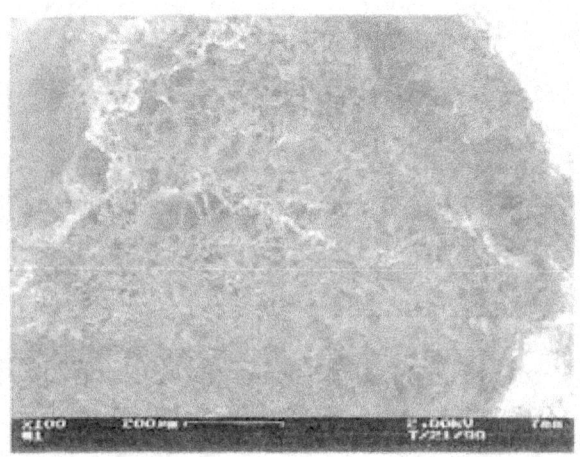
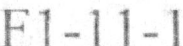

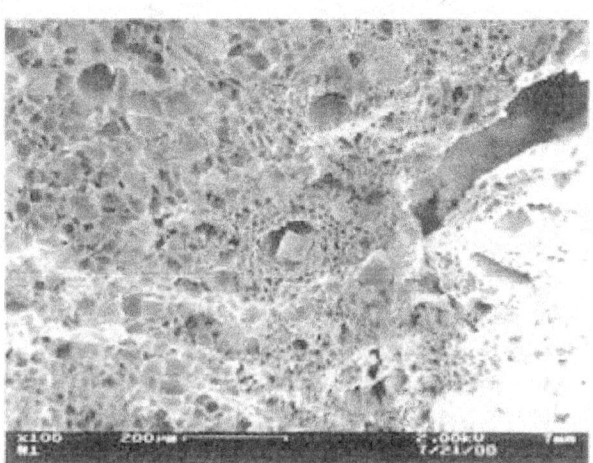

Figure 5.3 Photomicrographs of parenchymatous tissue samples

34

Fauna

by Tonya Largy

The high pH encountered in shell middens preserves bone in the normally acidic soils of northeastern North America. Preservation of all the bones originally deposited in a midden is, however, incomplete. Dogs and scavengers such as crows and herring gulls have ample opportunity to carry off freshly discarded food or other animal remains. A decade of personal observation of an open-air "midden" created with Largy kitchen scraps, including bone, demonstrates how quickly crows can remove the remains of a meal. Smaller, lightweight bones from birds like chicken are carried off immediately, certainly by the next morning. Heavier steak or chop bones may be left or carried to nearby locations, presumably by squirrels whose gnaw marks have been later observed. Therefore, a faunal assemblage provides only a sample of species that a site's inhabitants used.

Analysis was carried out using the comparative collections of the Zooarchaeology Laboratory, Peabody Museum, Harvard University, Cambridge, Massachusetts, and the collections of the ornithology, herpetology, molluscan, and ichthyology departments of the Museum of Comparative Zoology, Harvard University. Vertebrate fauna included mammal, bird, fish, salamander, and turtle. Mammal, bird, and larger fish bones were field collected while salamander, turtle, and numerous smaller fish, mammal, and bird bones were recovered through flotation. Most of the larger fragments can be identified as to genus and/or species, but most fragments from the flotation samples were extremely small in size and proved to be unidentifiable.

Molluscs

Large amounts of molluscs, or shellfish, were recovered from the 1999 flotation samples. Eastern oyster was the most numerous, followed by soft-shell clam. Very small fragments of ribbed mussel were present in every sample, and miniscule slipper shell, were also present. Numerous types of gastropods, or univalves, were also identified from the samples, all of which are believed to be land and brackish water marine snails that might be found in a marsh.

Mammal

Twenty-one mammal bones were recovered in all. Identified taxa include cow/ox, deer, dog, and rodent. Other fauna, while recovered, could not be identified to the particular taxa. Preservation of mammal bone, including one domesticated species (cow/ox), is likely due to relatively recent deposition and incorporation into the shell layer as a result of bioturbation.

Bird

Five bird taxa were present including bobwhite quail, canvasback duck, an immature pelican, bay duck, and a surface-feeding duck, whose exact taxa could not be identified. Most of the bird bones were recovered from Feature 1 in 1985.

Fish

A total of 74 fish bones were recovered. Most were fragmentary and unidentifiable, but three taxa were identified among the more complete specimens including oyster toadfish, white perch, and an individual from the cod family. The majority of the fish bone was recovered by flotation although none was large enough to identify. Flotation serves to eliminate recovery bias by showing that small fish were utilized, assuming their remains represent subsistence. The presence of small fish in the midden suggests this resource was a smaller dietary component, supplementing shellfish, bird, and mammal.

Amphibia

Salamander vertebrae identified as *Plethodon* sp. were recovered by flotation. These are likely naturally intrusive into the midden, but subsistence cannot be ruled out.

Reptiles

Turtles are represented by two carapace/plastron fragments recovered by flotation of samples from the 1999 units. These are very small fragments and bear no diagnostic landmarks. However, they are the first turtle remains to be recovered on Liberty Island.

Artifacts

by William Griswold

It was rather disappointing that more prehistoric artifacts were not discovered during the 1985 or the 1999 excavations. The archeologists who discovered and excavated Feature 1 in 1985 were extraordinarily lucky to find this feature and be given the chance to sample and date it. No lithic tools were recovered during the 1999 excavations and insufficient charcoal samples large enough to do a standard C-14 analysis were observed during the latest excavation. Only a handful of ceramics were found and the only projectile point was discovered in 1985. Dr. Elizabeth Chilton from the University of Massachusetts at Amherst aided us in the identification of the small number of artifacts.

One ceramic sherd from the 1985 excavation of Feature 1 (Cat. No. STLI-29681) was identified as a cord-marked, crushed quartz tempered fragment from the Middle Woodland period. One additional sherd (Cat. No. STLI-29723) and one projectile point (Cat. No. STLI –29724) were found in the western profile of the midden. Chilton identified the undecorated shell-tempered ceramic as belonging to the Middle Woodland Period. A jasper Levanna point, made from a flake was also recovered during the 1985 excavations.

Chilton additionally identified the ceramics recovered from the 1999 excavations as belonging to the Middle, Late, and very Late Woodland, possibly even the Contact Period. The ceramic fragments dating to the Middle and Late Woodland Period included Cat. Nos. STLI-30630 and STLI-30631. The very Late Woodland/Contact Period ceramics included Cat. No. STLI-30500. These findings suggest that the shell midden is a multi-component site, beginning in the Middle Woodland period and possibly continuing through the Contact period.

Figure 5.4 Photograph of a Woodland ceramic fragment

By undertaking controlled excavations like these, we can gather an understanding of what their environment was like and how Native Americans used their environment to meet their needs. Archeologists interpret what they find. But most of what we as humans do leaves no visible trace. It is very difficult to interpret beliefs, friendships, feelings, etc. However, by understanding a person's environment and how they used resources in it, we come that much closer to understanding the people we study.

Sources and Further Reading

There are several good textbooks on field methods in archeology. The classic one that the editor of this volume used during his school days is Martha Joukowsky's, *A Complete Manual of Field Archaeology: Tools and Techniques of Field Work for Archaeologists* (Englewood Cliffs, New Jersey, Prentice-Hall, Inc 1980). Another good one is T. R. Hester, H. J. Shafer, and K. L. Feder *Field methods in Archaeology* (Mountain View, Calif, Mayfield Publishing 1997). Many others exist and are equally well-written. These books will provide the interested reader the background information on field methodology.

Numerous reference works were consulted by the various authors to aid in the identification of faunal, floral, and material culture items. For paleobotanical identifications, references included R. M. Burns and B. H. Honkala, *Silvics of North America, Vol. I: Conifers & VoL II: Hardwoods* (Agricultural Handbook 654, USDA, Forest Service, Washington, D. C, 1990), F. Couplan, *The Encyclopedia of Edible Plants of North America* (Keats Publishing, New Caanan, Connecticut, 1998), J. K. Crellin and J. Philpott, *Reference guide to Medicinal Plants: Herbal Medicine Past and Present* (Duke University Press, Durham, 1989), K. Esau, *Anatomy of Seed Plants* (John Wiley & Sons, New York, 1966), A. Fahn, *Plant Anatomy,* Fourth Edition (Pergarnon Press,

Oxford, 1990)., J. G. Hather, "The Identification of Charred Archaeological Remains of Vegetative Parenchymatous Tissue" in *Journal of Archaeological Science* 18:661-675 (1991), and *A.n Archaeobotanical Guide to Root and Tuber Identification,* (Oxbow, Oxford 1993), R. B. Hoadley, *Identifying Wood: Accurate Results with Simple Tools,* (The Taunton Press, Newtown, Connecticut 1990), Lucinda McWeeney, "What Lies Lurking Below the Soil: Beyond the Archaeobotanical View of Flotation Samples (Mycorrhizal sclerotia)", *North American Archaeologist* 10(3):227-230 (1989). Other equally important works include D. E. Moerman, *Native American Ethnobotany,* (Timber Press, Portland 1998), D. Pearsall, *Paleoethnobotany* (Academic Press, New York 1989); F. H. Schweingruber, *Microscopic Wood Anatomy.* 3rd Edition. (Swiss Federal Institute for Forest, Snow and Landscape Research, Birmensdorf, Switzerland, 1978) and *Anatomy of European Woods* (Paul Haupt Publisher, Berne and Stuttgart, Birmsdorf, Switzerland 1990).

For faunal identifications, references consulted included Henry Bigelow and William Schroeder, *Fishes of the Gulf of Maine* (Fishery Bulletin of the Fish and Wildlife Service, Volume 53, USDA, Washington, 1953), S. C. Bishop, *Handbook of Salamanders* (Cornell University Press, Ithaca, New York 1943), John Bull, *.Birds of the New York State Area.* (Dover Publications, Inc., New York, 1975 reprint, first published in 1964, A. J. McClane (ed), *McLane's Standard Fishing Encyclopedia,* (Holt, Rinehart and Winston, New York, 1965), Edward Migdalski, *Salt Water Game Fishes* (The Ronald Press Company, New York 1958); Chandler Robbins, Bertel Bruun, and Herbert Zim, *Birds of North America* (Golden Press, New York. Holt, Rinehart and Winston, New York, 1983).

Information on the medieval warm period can be found in H. Lamb, "The Early

Medieval Warm Epoch and its Sequel" *Palaeogeography, Palaeoclimatology, Palaeoecology 1:* 13-37 (1965).

Numerous specialists were also consulted for the various identifications. Acknowledgments to these individuals can be found at the front of the book. Many of these individuals identified remains, which were not easily identifiable in books or articles.

CHAPTER SIX

WHAT ABOUT ALL OF THOSE BUILDINGS?

William Griswold

National Park Service, Northeast
Archeology Group

The maps gathered for the initial research showed that, at least during the historic period, buildings went up and came down with great speed. Landscape alterations that appeared on one map were absent from maps drawn just a few years later. Buildings also appeared in photographs that were never illustrated on maps. The maps obtained through the research project, while relatively numerous compared with other sites, only provide a snap shot of what was on the island during a particular year. Clearly, Liberty Island was a dynamic place, constantly undergoing changes in appearance.

At no time was the change more dramatic than when the entire island was placed under the control of the National Park Service. A master plan was developed soon after control of the island was given to the Park Service in 1937. This master plan began to be implemented in the late 1930s. Building demolition and landscape design continued into the 1940s, but progress slowed as the United States entered World War II. Following the war, work continued to complete the master plan. By the mid-1950s, the majority of the master plan had been accomplished. Later, just as Ms. Liberty was about to celebrate her first century, restoration work was begun on the statue and the island. The 1980s restoration work attempted to restore the statue's appearance and made numerous changes to the landscape of the island.

It was the changes done in the 1930s-1950s and in the 1980s that have had the biggest impact upon the archeology of the island. While photographs and drawings exist for some of these changes, they do not document all changes affecting the archeological landscape, nor can they always be trusted. In many cases the "as-built" drawings are either unavailable or unreliable. It was because so many changes have taken place on Liberty Island within the twentieth century that have not been documented that our options for archeological investigation were limited. It was difficult to determine what remained and what had long since vanished. The chosen option was to conduct a geophysical survey of the island and follow the geophysical investigations with archeological testing.

While records documenting all of the disturbances on the island were not available, certain historical documents provided hints as to what may be found. Carole Perrault's 1984 compilation provided many primary source documents illustrating and discussing the major landscape alterations on the island between 1871 and 1956. One of the most important visual records illustrating the changes that took place on the island is a *Pictorial Report for 1940*. This document provides 39 photographs illustrating the various changes that took place on the island between November 1, 1939 through December 1940

Figure 6.1 Arial photograph of the island during the 1940s demolition.

as a result of the WPA. During this time 8 buildings were demolished and eight of twelve acres of the island were graded. Walkways, steps, and retaining walls were also constructed around the island and construction was begun on the administration and concessions buildings. The photographs provide an excellent visual record of the demolition work.

The difficulty in using this document is that many of the figure labels are ambiguous. For example one photograph labeled March 29, 1940 reads "The basement walls remained until March when work began under the new project." The following photograph, taken on June 1, 1940, is labeled "The basement was filled to subgrade." Questions arise as to what happened to the walls and floor of the building. Were the walls removed? Did the basement have a stone/concrete or earthen floor? If it had a constructed floor, was the floor removed? Some of the figure labels mention the removal of basements. For example a figure label on a photograph taken on March 22, 1940 reads "The removal of the basements of the hospital

building and Building #21 began under the new project." It is doubtful then, that anything archeological remains on these two buildings.

LOCATION OF TEST PITS

The same surveying equipment used for the previous work was used in 2000 to stake out the various test pits. Small, object oriented anomalies were not chosen for investigation. Rather the work of the 2000 season concentrated on the evaluation of large anomalies such as the confirmation of stratigraphic horizons, former structures, filled depressions, and dipping reflectors.Previous experience has taught me that geophysical investigations, while technologically advanced, are not always reliable. As a result, test pits were placed both inside and outside the anomalies identified by the geophysicists. This provided comparative data inside and outside the anomalies. While slightly more than seventy test pits were laid out, only fifty-five were excavated. This was because stratification in many of the units was very deep and time consuming to excavate.

THE RESULTS

The plethora of strata uncovered during excavation on Liberty Island, make it difficult to interpret. The multitude of photos of the island throughout the last 100 + years show how quickly landscape and building alterations are made. These alterations, no doubt, account for much of what was uncovered during the 2000 excavations. While some of these deposits were large in extent, many were very small. Most of the changes are suspected to be

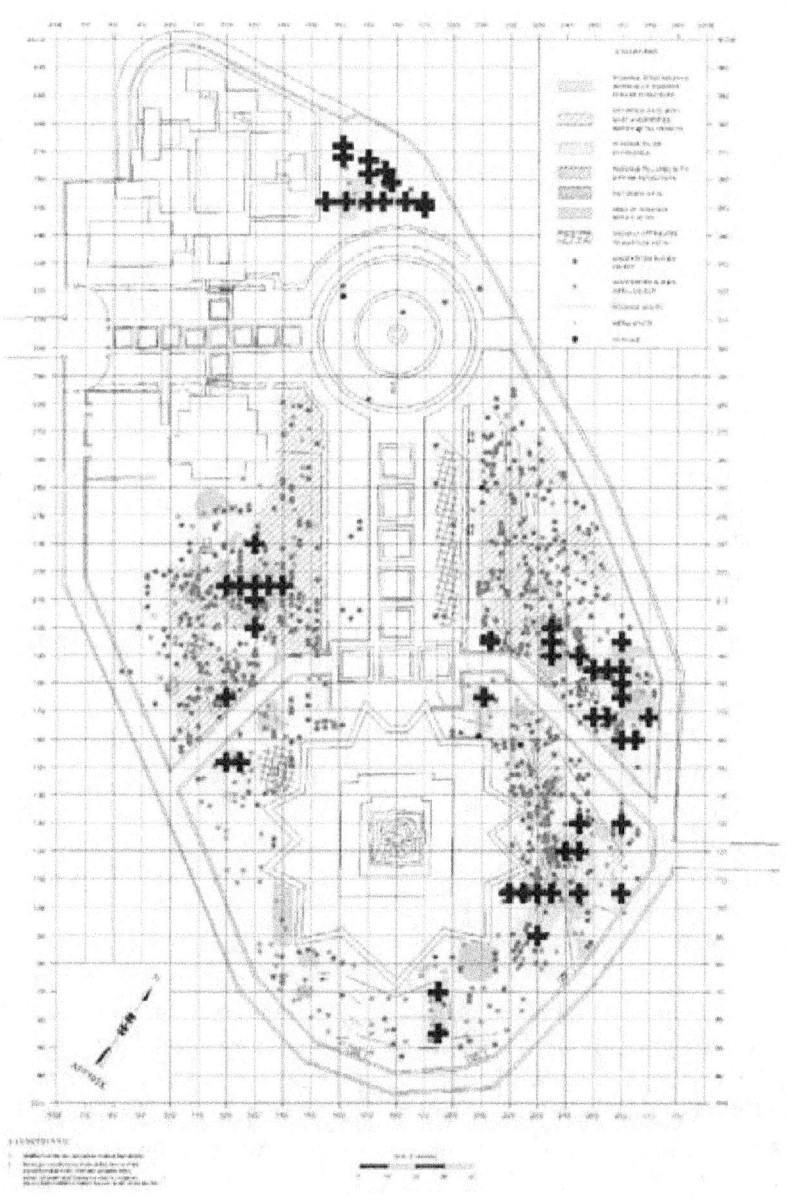

Figure 6.2 Location of units excavated in 2000.

relatively innocuous layers associated with either the construction or destruction of a building or the creation of the formal landscape connected with the park. Many of these layers do not require interpretation, and in many cases may not be open to interpretation, especially given the small size of the exposure. Most of the artifacts recovered from the deposits lend little information about their deposition. Coal, brick fragments, and mortar fragments were by far the most numerous artifacts recovered.

Several maps, gathered from various sources and entered into a GIS program, have been included with this chapter. Geographical Information System or GIS referes to computer programs that allow people to view geographic information. GIS was very useful for this project, because all of the maps gathered during the initial research could be scanned and layered in a file. By doing this, we were able to look at the overlays of various maps. The composite maps developed from these sources were then used to make some interpretations. There are, however, certain problems inherent with using these maps.

Most of these maps were drawn without the accuracy available in modern surveys. Errors are common when one map is laid on top of another. None of the maps match exactly. At times some of the maps must be stretched or twisted. While these maps generally conform to one another, errors of a few meters are not uncommon. Therefore, one must always be mindful of this when using the maps to interpret the excavations.

Another problem with the maps is they represent the configuration of the island at one point in time. We don't have a map that shows all of the buildings and all of the changes that happened to the island. In total, we have representations of the island at approximately 20 points in time. In reality, many, if not most, of the changes of the island are not represented.

The North end of the island

The north end of the island was one of the most fruitful areas for accessible archeological resources. Most of the maps were not helpful in interpreting the strata or artifacts found. However, the 1936 map provides some information for interpreting the strata found and has been reproduced with the overlays as Figure 6.3. A cement floor to an undocumented building was found in two adjacent units (N352 E162 and N 352 E 170). Since the 1900 map of the island shows the location of this cement floor to be in a tidal zone, it must post date 1900. Remnants of other buildings were also found. While the bottom of unit N352 E175 was never reached, several of the strata were clearly construction fill, probably in Building 15, according to the 1937 map. The Non-Commissioned Officer's Quarters, as the building is described in the 1937 Master Plan, was a two-story brick building housing two families. No mention is made of a basement, even though the entries for other buildings contain references to a basement. The sloping nature of the fill evident in these deposits, along with the coarse nature of the material encountered in them (brick, limestone, etc.) leads one to believe that these deposits represent the filling of a building, with at least a crawl space below.

While the location of N367 E170 seems to be just south of the location of the radio tower building (Building 22) on the 1936 map, the coarse fill, the concrete, and the large voids seem to indicate that this is what remains of the building. The building is described in the 1937 Master Plan as a one-story brick building with an attic and a basement. This radio tower building was supposedly established in 1905 or 1906 according to the 1937 Master Plan.

The hard-packed earth encountered in N368 E161 (Stratum 3) and N372 E161 (Stratum 3) are probably the result of the compression of soil from the radio tower and radio tower pad resting on top of them. The date of the tower, according to the master plan is uncertain. The lower stratum within the unit, contained brick with "S & F Co." impressed upon them, a local brick making company operating in the late nineteenth and early twentieth centuries.

The location of N352 E183 appears to be just outside of the Non-Commissioned Officer's Quarters, described above. It appears to be underneath a porch on the back of the house. Stratum 4 in N352 E183 was described as medium density gravel. Gravel is commonly used below porches for drainage.

Building and remnants of buildings were not the only archeological resources found. Examples of some of the material used to construct walkways (pea-gravel and coal ash) were also found in some of the units (N352 E162, N352 E155), indicating that some vestiges of the earlier pre-NPS landscape still exist.

The east side of the island

An extensive earlier ground surface was found in 12 of the 16 units excavated (Figure 6.2). This earlier ground surface was

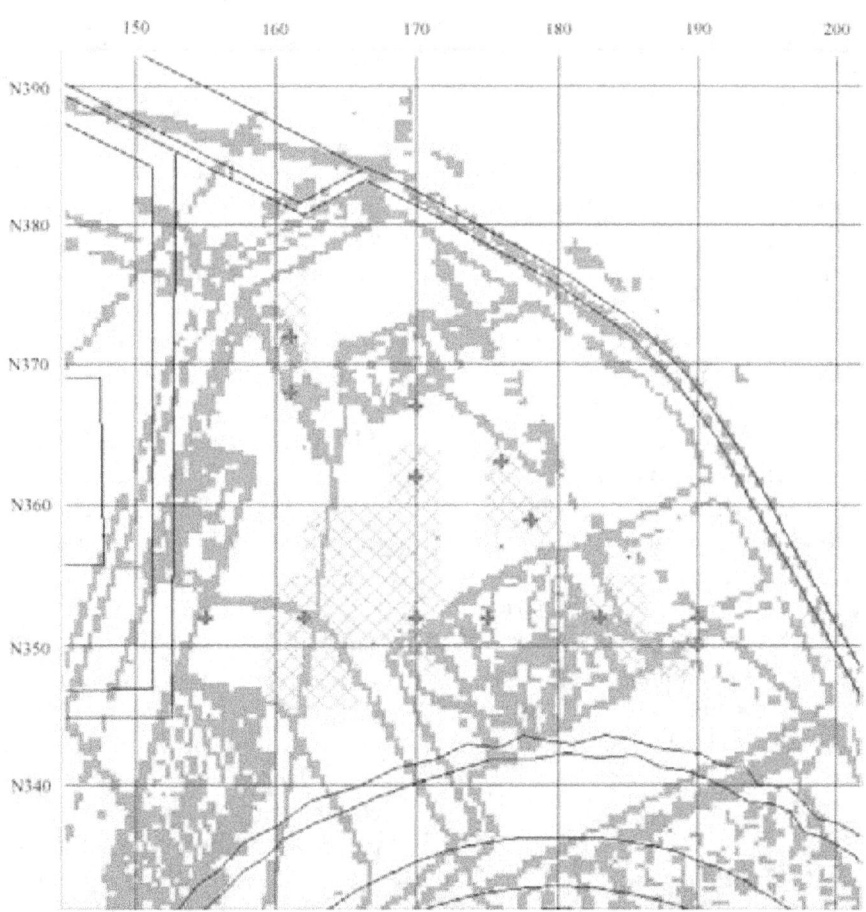

Figure 6.3 Overlays of various maps and test pit locations at the North end of the island

composed primarily of very compacted clay but contained few artifacts. It was at least 30 cms lower than the current ground surface in almost all of the units, but seems to be more deeply buried to the east. This compact stratum is probably the reason for the geophysical anomaly. While testing confirmed the existence of the anomaly well inside the defined area, the earlier ground surface was also found in units outside of the defined boundary. Figure 6.2 indicates that this earlier ground surface was found in numerous units where, until 1939-1940, there was an Officer's Quarters building, a building which had a basement. Therefore, the earlier ground surface must post-date the destruction and backfilling of the building. It is very likely, then that this is the earlier ground surface is connected with the park and likely deposited between 1940 and 1985.

In many of the excavated units, excavation and coring proved inconclusive in determining what was sandy fill and what was true geological subsoil or naturally deposited sand. It seems, however, that true geological subsoil was confined to four units (N185 E250, N190 E235, N195 E213, and N195 E235). The elevation associated with the subsoil in these units indicates a moderate slope from approximately 1.0-meter to .13 meters over approximately 7.5 meters. The slope in the subsoil is probably responsible for the geophysical anomaly. Hager-Richter defined the area around two of the units as "possible fill areas with dipping reflectors." The dipping reflectors probably relate to the slope of the subsoil. It seems then that the sand found in the other units was fill.

The west side of the island

It was clear from the excavations conducted in 1999 that the subsoil sloped rather dramatically from east to west, beginning at the hedgerow. Subsoil was not confirmed in any of the units excavated on the west side during the 2000 season. The viewing of the various historic maps in ArcView shows that much of this part of the island is composed of fill. The 2000 excavations confirmed this.

An earlier ground surface was also found on the west side of the island, and is no doubt the geophysical anomaly identified by Hager-Richter. Like the former ground surface identified on the eastern side of the island, this compacted clay layer contained few artifacts to date the deposit. However, Figure 6.3 clearly shows the former ground surface extending over the area formerly occupied by the Non-commissioned Officer's Quarters building (Number 21). According to a 1940 photograph, this building had a basement. Even the very deep excavation of N215 E120 did not find the bottom of the basement at 1.5 meters below the surface. The former ground surface must then post-date the destruction of the building and its subsequent filling. It was probably the previous ground surface between 1940 and 1985. A reddish colored clay loam had been deposited over the area as part of the 1980's rehabilitation of the statue.

The south end of the island

Subsoil was located in several of the units immediately around the outside perimeter of the fort walls (N70 E195, N105 E225, N105 E230, N152 E120, N152 E125, and N175 E211). It was unusual that the geophysical testing did not locate the ditch surrounding the fort. However, further research in 2000 indicated that in 1904 the War Department had graded away the counterscarp down to the bottom of the ditch to provide fill for building construction on the north end of the island. This explains why relatively modern material was found on top of the subsoil near the fort walls.

A large rubble fill deposit was encountered in N105 E235 and N105 E245. This rubble fill, and the fact that subsoil was never reached within either of these units, may indicate that it is fill within a building. No structure in this position was found on any of the historic maps. An earlier ground surface was likewise detected sporadically across the area. Undoubtedly, this ground surface probably dates to the same period as the other ground surfaces found across the site, namely 1940-1985.

By far the most interesting discovery this season was the continuation of the historic midden deposits, first uncovered in the 1999 season. These deposits contain artifacts of a late eighteenth/very early nineteenth-century date, and thus predate the construction of Fort Wood. They were deposited on top of the prehistoric midden deposits previously discussed. The results of the analysis of the faunal material collected from the 1999 excavations indicate that the animal remains within the midden deposit are more reminiscent of military consumption than household consumption. In some cases a relatively thick deposit of sand was spread over the historic midden deposits. It is logical to conclude that the thick sand layer is the spoil from the excavation of the ditch around Fort Wood. Several fortification features would have been created using the spoil including a counterscarp and a glacis (see glossary). The remaining sand deposits are likely the only remnants of these features with most of the soil used to construct them being relocated to the northern end of the island.

ADDING TO THE HISTORY

During the 1999 excavations on the prehistoric shell midden, deposits from a late 18th/early 19th-century midden were also

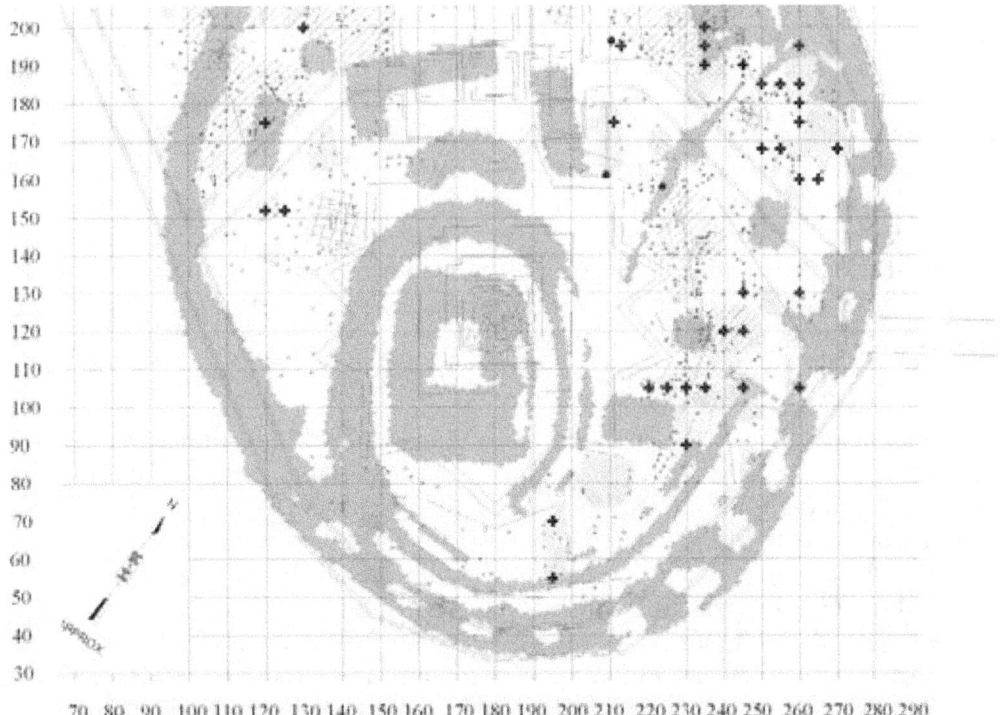

Figure 6.4 A portion of the 1766 map overlaid by the geophysical testing map and the 2000 excavations.

discovered. These midden deposits overlay the prehistoric shell midden and were spread out over a much larger area. A variety of late eighteenth/early nineteenth century ceramics were discovered including several examples of pearlware and creamware. More will be said later about the ceramics and the other artifacts found in this historic midden deposit. Field collected fauna recovered from the historic midden deposits, however, provides unique insight into the early dietary habits of the early military inhabitants.

Fauna

by Tonya Barody Largy and Sarah E. Whitcher, Ph.D.

The faunal remains analyzed here were collected from several test units excavated in the historic midden in 1999. The primary goal of this portion of the project was to identify and analyze the fauna. A secondary goal of the analysis was to see if the faunal pattern was more likely the result of domestic or military consumption. In other words, were the bones the result of meals eaten by the residents of the island, or by the soldiers? If you will recall from Chapter 2, Liberty Island was home to both residents and soldiers during the later 18th/early 19th-century. The archeologists could not precisely date the midden deposit because too few artifacts were found. These deposits were however covered by a sand deposit, of varying thickness, believed to be from the excavation of the ditch surrounding Fort Wood built for the War of 1812.

The analyzed assemblage comes from soil sifted through the standard ¼ inch hardware cloth. As a result, many of the small fish bones were not present. Bulk soil samples were collected during the 1999 season, but flotation has not yet been done for these deposits. When analyzed these bulk samples may provide additional data on

smaller bones that would have passed through the screen.

Analysis was carried out primarily by Sarah Whitcher, Research Assistant, Zooarchaeology Laboratory of the Peabody Museum, Harvard University, working in conjunction with Tonya Largy. Identifications were made using the comparative collection of the Zooarchaeology Laboratory, supplemented by mammal, bird and fish collections in the Harvard Museum of Natural History. Dr. Douglas Causey, Senior Vertebrate Biologist was especially helpful with bird identifications. Mr. Peter Burns, also on staff at the Zooarchaeology Laboratory, assisted with the identification of fish bone. Bone was examined both with and without a microscope. A microscope was used to identify chop/cut/saw marks, burning, and gnawing by carnivores or rodents.

Just under 400 bones were examined during the analysis of the 1999 Liberty Island collection. Because of the small size of many of the faunal fragments, few were identified to the genus/species level. Of the identified bones, 22 were cattle, 11 were sheep/goat, 2 were pig, 7 were birds, 2 were deer, and 5 were fish. While all of the faunal remains could not be precisely identified, most could be placed into a taxonomic class (eg. mammal, bird, fish).

Domestic Mammals

Cattle constituted the largest number of identifiable remains. While the sample size is relatively small, many things can still be said about the dietary habits of the people who ate them. For example, studies have shown that cattle provide the highest quality of beef between 1.5 to 3 years of age. Age can be inferred on bones based on a few key indicators like the fusion of the long bones. Long bones, like a person's upper arm or upper leg, are actually unfused when a person is young. When a person matures, the ends of the bones, known as epiphyses, grow together or fuse with the long shaft of the bone, known as the diaphysis. The same happens in mammals. The calculated ages for the Liberty Island cattle bones suggest that at least some of the animals were outside the prime age for butchery. The inhabitants of the island responsible for the deposition of the bones ate a few cattle younger than 1.5 years and a few older than 3 years.

An analysis of body parts can also tell us something about food preferences and diet. The only animal from Liberty Island for which body part analysis is possible is cattle. The overwhelming majority (91%) of the bones are from high meat-yielding body parts (back, ribs, and upper limbs). Head and foot bones, low meat-yield areas, constitute only a small percentage of the remains (9%).

This pattern indicates that the midden contains food refuse, rather than butchery refuse, in which case we would expect to find many more head and foot bones. However, it is still not clear how the meat was obtained. The large number of high meat-yielding bones and near absence of head and foot refuse suggests that the meat was obtained already butchered. On the other hand, butchery may have taken place somewhere else on the island.

Body part analysis also suggests that upper forelimb bones (scapula, humerus, radius/ulna) are nearly twice as numerous as hindlimb bones (pelvis, femur, tibia). This may indicate a dietary preference for forelimb cuts, and is further support for the meat being obtained in a butchered form (rather than butchered on the site).

Other than cattle, no other taxa had enough bones to make a statistically valid comparison. However, it is interesting to note that the majority of sheep/goat bones are upper limb and back bones, with a few ankle bones and one tooth. As in cattle, there were no toe bones suggesting that these were removed in butchery that was either at another location in the vicinity, or even before the meat was purchased.

Wild Mammals

The only bones of wild mammals found in the historic midden were two foot bones of white-tailed deer. A few of the unidentified bones may be from a deer, but the fragments could not be identified with certainty. Almost certainly, venison would have been transported to the island. Given the small size of the island (about 8 acres at this time), there would have been insufficient habitat for a permanent herd. However, deer are known to swim between islands to browse and this animal may have been captured while browsing on the island. It is more likely, however, that portions of deer were brought in for food in much the same way that beef cuts were supplied to the people living on the island.

Birds

Only 3% of all the bones from the historic midden were identified as bird. Two types of birds were represented in the analyzed fauna: chicken and Tundra swan (*Cygnus columbianus*). Native Tundra swans are not commonly seen in the northeast but were more numerous in earlier times. In fact, the Tundra Swan may have frequently visited the mid-Atlantic coast in the 17th and 18th centuries during the Little Ice Age, when cooler temperatures prevailed.

Fish

A total of 36 fish bones were identified, but only five bones (2%) are identified to the species. Four bones were identified as striped bass, and one bone was from a Red drum. Both striped bass and red drum would have been available in the marketplace or caught in the harbor.

DISCUSSION

Although the 1999 excavation of the historic midden on Liberty Island resulted in a relatively small sample of bone, trends are unmistakable. Clearly, the dominant species in the assemblage is cattle with lesser representations of sheep/goat and pigs. Domestic and wild species are both represented. Shellfish were also gathered and eaten by these people, but none of the shellfish were analyzed. It was clear, however, from the 1999 excavations that shellfish were also part of the diet.

It is unknown when the house was built, but by 1753 there was a house and a lighthouse on the island and a variety of food sources were available to the residents. An advertisement, listed in Stokes, to rent the property in the 18th-century illustrates some of the rich dietary resources that the island offered.

> "Bedloe's Island, alias Love Island", if offered to let, "together with the Dwelling-House and Light-House, being finely situated for a Tavern, where all kind of Garden Stuff, Poultry, &c may be easily raised for the Shipping, outward bound and from whence any Quantity of pickled Oysters may be transported; it abounds with English Rabbits"

One way to evaluate the patterning seen in the Liberty Island historic faunal assemblage is to look at other sites where comparable faunal analysis has been done. Fort Stanwix, a French and Indian War and Revolutionary War site in Rome, New York had excavation done on it in the early 1970s by Lee Hanson and Dick Hsu. The results of these investigations are available in the book entitled *Casemates and Cannonballs*. The Fort Stanwix assemblage was dominated by cattle. Pig and deer were equally represented while chicken, fish and wild birds were represented along with several wild mammals and reptiles. The strong presence of deer and other wild mammals can be explained by the fort's location in a rural, forested area with a rich resource base during the period of occupation.

A faunal assemblage from the mid-19th century Fort Fillmore, New Mexico, analyzed by Parmalee also provides comparable data to ours from Liberty Island. Parmalee found that the main source of food was beef, with sheep/goat and pig in small numbers. Interestingly, he suggested that pork might have been brought in as cured meat, explaining the near absence of pig bones (even though texts indicate that the occupants of the fort ate bacon). Parmalee also found an absence of head and foot bones, which he attributed to slaughter occurring at a different location (and that the fort did not have its own herds).

The military probably also brought in beef quarters to Liberty Island since the island would not provide enough space for cattle, although pigs and chickens might be kept easily. The above advertisement to rent the house offers only the potential for raising poultry and garden produce. It also mentions the island "abounds with English rabbits". Presumably, pigs also could be kept. The absence of rabbit bones in the assemblage suggests the rabbits were completely gone by the time the midden was deposited.

The overwhelming number of cattle bones points away from a domestic context for these bones. Domestic contexts would likely find more pigs, sheep/goats, and chickens. For example, the most numerous taxon represented at the Spencer-Pierce-Little Farm in Newbury, Massachusetts was pig followed by cattle, sheep/goat, pigeon/rock dove, and chicken. Additionally, a domestic context would likely produce butchery discard (in the form of head and foot bones), especially from smaller domestic mammals and birds. However, it is possible that butchery refuse was deposited elsewhere and was not retrieved in this excavation.

Both Parmalee's and Hanson and Hsu's results from military contexts parallel our results from Liberty Island and present a good argument for an association with the late 18th/early 19th-century military occupation. The bones could either be the food remains of British soldiers during the Revolution or American soldiers when the island was fortified in 1794.

The Artifacts

By William Griswold

Several noteworthy artifacts were found during both the 1999 and 2000 seasons. While the 1999 season concentrated on uncovering the prehistoric resources of the island some historic artifacts were also uncovered. However, many more historic artifacts were discovered in 2000, when

ground-truthing the geophysical investigations took place.

Several interesting military buttons were found during the 2000 excavations. Since I am not an expert in the identification of buttons, I turned to Hughes' and Lester's the *Big Book of Buttons*. By using this reference manual, I was able to identify several buttons. One (STLI-33053) was an infantry officer's button. While no exact parallels could be found for this button, Hughes and Lester illustrate one on page 716 with many similar features. Another one (STLI-35162) contains an eagle clutching branches with a "US" in the middle. The words "United States Infantry" are depicted in raised lettering around the edge on the obverse of the button. No date or manufacturer could be assigned to this button. Still another button (STLI-33832 not illustrated) was identified by Hughes and Lester as a Light Artillery button dating between 1808 and 1814. They go on to describe the light artillery as being created in 1808 and absorbed into the regular

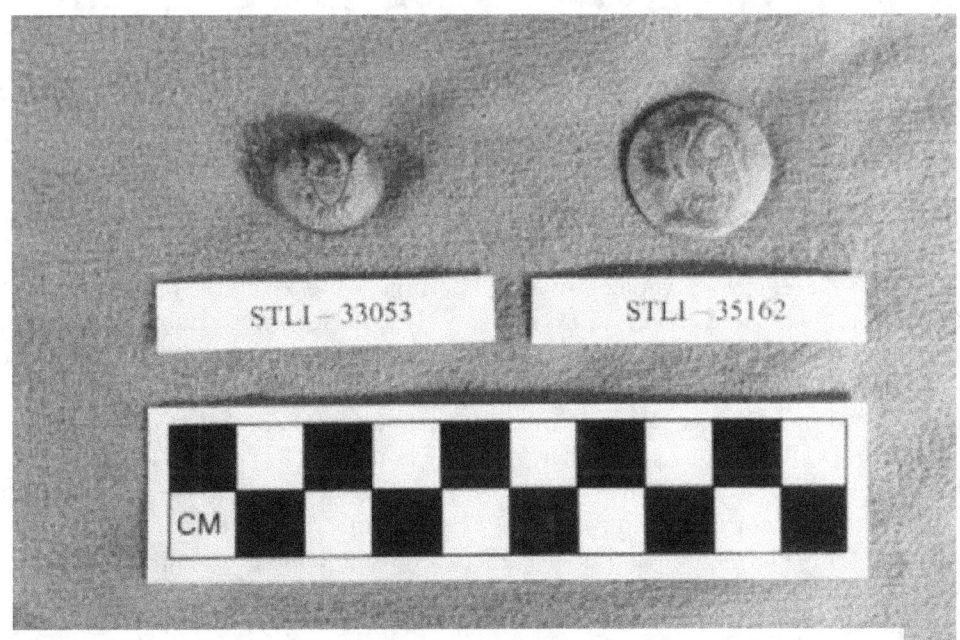

Figure 6.5 Two military buttons found during the excavations.

49

regimental structure of the army in 1821 (716-717).

Several tobacco pipe fragments were also found during the excavations. These were all made of kaolin, a white clay. One important characteristic of tobacco pipes, both stems and bowls, is that they undergo regular changes in design and

contexts for their importance in identifying children in the archeological record. However, marbles were not solely restricted to children. Adults often used them as gaming pieces. The context in which STLI-34652 was found was not as informative as if it had been found on a regular domestic site where we could infer the user, the status

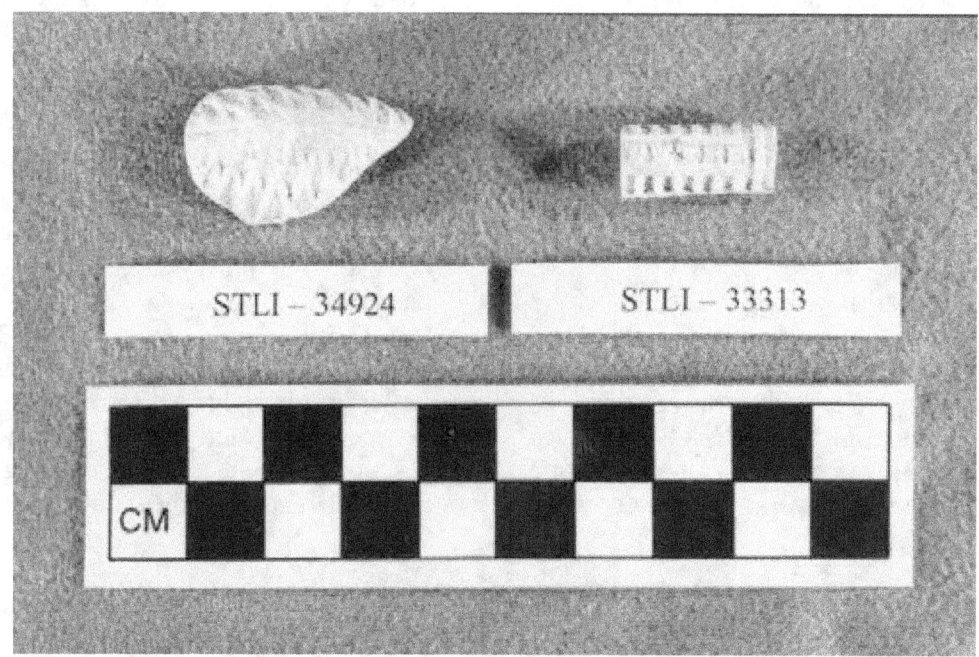

Figure 6.6 Tobacco pipe fragments found during the excavations.

construction. One bowl fragment (STLI-34924) was decorated by a raised, molded weave pattern on the exterior. Another two fragments (STLI-33313 and STLI-33934) contained either the full or partial rendering of the name "PETER DORNI" with "PETER" in raised molding on one side of the stem and "DORNI" on the other. Identical examples have been found and published elsewhere. According to Omwake, Peter Dorni was a widely-imitated French pipemaker ca. 1850 whose pipes were exported to the US.

One small, round clay marble (STLI-34652) was excavated from N352 E162. Marbles have been noted in other

of the user's family, etc. Without further study (trace element analysis) it is impossible to tell the origin of this marble.

Several ceramic fragments were found during the 2000 excavations that deserve comment. Attribution of origin is tentative for several of these ceramics. Three examples (STLI-35051) collected on the surface at the north end of the island appear to come from the same vessel and contain both shell and grit temper. They appear to be poorly made European ceramics. Another fragment (STLI-35077) is much more refined and appears to be of European origin, possibly Dutch, although this attribution is very tentative. This fragment also came from the northern end of the island. One prehistoric ceramic fragment (STLI-35222) is shell tempered with fiber or grass impressions evident. It is a product of incomplete or uncontrolled firing as the interior and exterior sides are reddish brown in color while the body of the fragment is black. It is notable that this fragment was found mixed in with historic period deposits on the northern end of the island.

Carole Perrault in her 1984 compendium cites a 1904 letter from G. C. Burnell, Captain, Signal Corps, U.S.A to the Adjutant General, Department of the East, Governor's Island, N.Y. In this letter, Burnell indicates that "a certain amount of filling will be required on [the north] end of the Island. To provide dirt for this purpose and generally improve the grounds it is recommended that the counterscarp and glacis on the north side of the Statue be cut down to the level of the moat." This is precisely the area where the prehistoric and early historic middens are located. I would argue that the early material that was located on the north end of the island has been relocated from its original position near the location of the midden.

As one can see, Liberty Island has been slow to reveal her past. Archeological excavation has illustrated that key spots on the island have enormous potential for illuminating the past, while other areas tell us little that we don't already know. Separating the wheat from the chaff, however, is what archeology is all about. Continued archeological projects on the island will inevitably reveal additional information about the cultural land use practices on the island.

Sources and Further Reading

Several sources were consulted for the interpretation of the faunal remains. These included, Lee Hanson and Dick Ping Hsu, *Casemates and Cannonballs*: *Archaeological Investigations at Fort Stanwix National Monument, Rome, New York*. (Publications in Archeology 14. U.S. Department of the Interior, National Park Service, Washington, D.C. 1975); David Landon, Feeding Colonial Boston: a Zooarchaeologal Study. *Historical Archaeology* 30 (1):1-153 (1996); Paul W. Parmalee, Food animals utilized by the garrison stationed at Fort Fillmore, New Mexico 1851-1862. *El Palacio*. 74 (2):43-45 (1967); I. A. Silver, "The ageing of domestic animals" in *Science and Archaeology*, edited by D. Brothwell and E. Higgs, pp. 283-302. (Thames & Hudson, London 1969).

Two sources used for the identification of the historic artifacts were E. Hughes and M. Lester, *The Big book of Buttons* (second printing), (J.S. McCarthy Company, Augusta, Maine, 1991) and H. Geiger Omwake, "Analysis of 19th century White Kaolin Pipe Fragments from the Mero Site, Door County, Wisconsin," in *Wisconsin Archaeologist* 26 (N.S.), No. 2 (1965).

Background information on the development of the island, at least for the purposes of this chapter comes from two sources. Carole Perrault's, "The Statue of Liberty and Liberty Island: A Chronicle of the Physical Conditions and Appearance of the Island, 1871-1956" Manuscript on file at the National Park Service, Northeast Cultural Resources Center, Lowell, Massachusetts (1984), I. N. P. Stokes, *The Iconography of Manhattan Island* (New York: Robert Dodd 1928) and the *Pictorial Report for 1940*.

CHAPTER SEVEN

WHAT DOES IT ALL MEAN?

William Griswold

National Park Service, Northeast
Archeology Group

THE PREHISTORIC MIDDEN DEPOSITS

Given the amount of construction activity that has taken place on Liberty Island, it is difficult for many to believe that an archeological resource as valuable as a prehistoric shell midden could still be preserved, although other prehistoric sites have been found in equally unlikely contexts. The prehistoric shell midden was not only preserved, but yielded a plethora of information concerning Native American life, especially as it unfolded in the last two millennium. It was likely preserved due to the original topography of the island; according to the 1766 map, the site seems to be in a depressed area of the island.

The radiocarbon dates taken from the pre-midden Feature 1 suggest a radio-carbon date of approximately 1000 years ago. This correlates to the end of the Middle Woodland Period or the beginning of the Late Woodland Period. Radiocarbon dates have not been done on the shell from the site. This date of corresponds to a time when peoples were heavily utilizing coastal resources throughout the Northeast coastal region. These studies, as well as the data from the Liberty Island site, indicate that a wide diversity of food resources was available to the Native American population. It seems that plant domestication was much more important on the interior where resources were more limited.

The ceramic fragments found within the shell midden during the 1999 season, clearly show that the shell midden was formed as a result of shellfish exploitation during several prehistoric periods, beginning in the Middle Woodland, continuing through the Late Woodland, and possibly even extending into the Contact period. Since the shells of the midden were deposited over Feature 1 (1985) it is assumed that the C-14 dates obtained from the feature represent the earliest prehistoric dates for this portion of the site. However, we can't rule out that older areas of the midden may have existed, but have been destroyed during construction activities at the site. We may find some older material on the island someday, but for now the oldest prehistoric deposits seem date back just about 1000 years ago.

While oyster remains account for the largest percentage of identified molluscs in the site, Largy's analysis indicates that numerous other shellfish, fin fish, mammal, bird, reptiles, and amphibia are represented within the shell midden. These include softshell clam, ribbed mussel, slipper shell, a host of identified univalves, deer, dog, rodents, several unidentifiable large, medium, and small mammals, bobwhite quail, canvasback duck, bay duck, other duck, an immature pelican, oyster toadfish, white perch, cod-family fish, salamander, and turtle. Some identified taxa, i.e. cow, are intrusive into the earlier deposits.

Largy has cogently argued elsewhere that the discovery of a fledgling/nestling pelican bone may indicate a climatic warming. The bones of the pelican were found in Feature 1 (1985) and the charcoal in the feature has been radiocarbon dated to the end of the Middle Woodland/beginning of the Late Woodland. These birds do not normally nest this far north. For these birds to nest this far north, the temperature would have been warmer than at present. Lucinda McWeeney and David Perry have additionally noted that around A.D. 1000 the "Little Climatic Warming Period" was occurring and had allowed several trees to extend their northern range into the coastal New York and Connecticut regions.

Several species of flora are also represented in the midden. Wood fragments oak, elm, juniper, and possibly other coniferous and deciduous trees. A relatively large number of charred hickory nutshell indicates the choice of this nut as for food. Parenchymatous tissue analysis also identified water lily and flowering rush, two freshwater plants. This discovery raises some interesting questions, especially since the earliest maps of the island show no fresh water source. The most reasonable conclusion is that these plants were brought to the island when the shellfish were collected, indicating that these people were likely making multiple stops for the procurement of various resources during their hunting and gathering forays. An alternate suggestion is that the plants were growing in a nearby freshwater pond now inundated by saltwater.

In addition to being used during several of the prehistoric periods, the evidence also shows that the island was likely used during several seasons of the year. Not all of the flora and fauna identified from the excavations are available during one season. It seems, however, that the late summer/fall season was an important time to come to Liberty Island to collect various fauna and flora. The lack of any long-term features connected with the midden seem to indicate that the forays to Liberty Island were just short-term trips and that the Native Americans may not have lived on the island for long periods. Another possible interpretation may be that Native Americans did live on the island, but those features which would be associated with long-term habitation have been destroyed.

The discovery of a jasper Levanna projectile point during the 1985 excavations indicates that the Native Americans were utilizing regional (area available and not island available) resources for their lithic tools; the only raw materials available on the site are those materials that wash up on shore. While a small number of flakes were uncovered during the 1999 season, lithic production or reduction seems to have been a relatively minor activity on the site.

It must again be pointed out that the formation processes on shell middens are complex. While it can not unequivocally be stated that all of the flora and fauna species identified in the analysis of the midden come from human exploitation of those species, the analysis suggests a diverse diet, utilizing numerous estuarine, riverine, and terrestrial resources.

THE HISTORIC DEPOSITS

The discovery of a large deposit of late eighteenth/early nineteenth century midden material during the 1999 and 2000 seasons is indeed surprising. It is very likely that the material contained within the midden predates the construction of Fort Wood, since a deposit of sand of varying thickness, covers the midden deposits and is believed to be related to the construction of the ditch and the glacis around Fort Wood. The design and construction of Fort Wood in the early nineteenth century was part of a larger harbor defense plan developed and overseen by Col. Jonathan Williams.

The evidence garnered from the faunal analysis conducted on the bones recovered from the midden suggests that the fauna were left by soldiers. The fact that the remains consist primarily of cow remains and the fact that only certain parts of the cow were found illustrate this point. The question then remains, what soldiers and from where. Liberty Island was fortified and occupied before the Fort Wood fortifications were constructed. The presence of creamware, pearlware, and a variety of imported stoneware and probable glacis deposits covering the midden necessarily limit the time of deposit to between 1760 and 1808. During this time the British occupied the island during part of the Revolution and housed Tory refugees and later in the 1790s the Americans constructed earthen fortifications on the island. The remains contained in the midden could be from either group. The only way to really clarify the situation is to do more excavation.

The Fort Wood Remains

The excavations conducted in 2000 showed that at least some fragments of the buildings from the Fort Wood period remain. The area at the north end of the island, which is currently off limits to the visitors, seems especially promising. The 2000 excavations in this area document the remains of buildings and the filling of some of the foundations and basements with debris. This debris encountered within the foundations is probably from the walls having been pushed into the foundations as much of the rubble fill encountered in the excavations was very course. Often this rubble consisted of whole bricks with the mortar still adhering to them, sometimes joined with other bricks.

The area at the north end of the island would be a good place to investigate because the remains are fairly close to the surface. The fill encountered within the

buildings on the east and west sides of the island was often buried much deeper and consisted primarily of sand. Some of the basements of these buildings, including the floors, may be preserved but are buried deeper than 3 meters. If you will remember, 3 meters is the approximate lower-end limit for many of the geophysical investigations. Investigating archeological deposits or features on the island that are buried 3 meters or more is logistically difficult. Usually, a large area must be opened and the sides of the excavation must be supported to prevent collapse.

One should also consider the value of an excavation designed to search for the deeply buried remains of Fort Wood buildings. The photographs taken during the demolition of many of the buildings show all of the above ground portion of the walls dismantled with only the footprint of the building remaining. Based on the limited excavations that we did in these buildings, it seems that, if they were filled, they may have been filled with rather clean fill. In other words, if someone were to excavate in these old buildings, they may find the cement floor of the building and perhaps a few artifacts dating to the time of the demolition of the building. This may or may not be a valuable archeological endeavor. The construction of many of these buildings, however, would certainly have destroyed any earlier deposits or artifacts that would have been buried below the footprint.

Early Statue of Liberty Deposits

During the 2000 excavations several deposits were discovered which date to the first official landscape design (1930s) of the island. In many cases, these deposits were composed of densely packed clay. Few artifacts were discovered during the excavation of these deposits. While relatively young, these deposits may have National Register Significance because of their association with Norman Newton, an early renowned National Park Service Landscape Architect.

Sources and Further Reading

Most of the information contained in this chapter comes from unpublished excavation reports. One monograph has come out, however, that discusses the discoveries made when the shell midden was excavated. This book, intended primarily for scholars, was edited by William Griswold and is titled, *Archeology of a Prehistoric Shell Midden, Statue of Liberty National Monument, New York* (Archeology Branch, Northeast Region, National Park Service, 2002). A limited number of copies were printed for distribution. This volume, however, contains contributions by Lucinda McWeeney, David Perry, and Tonya Largy that discuss the discoveries in great detail.

CHAPTER EIGHT

WHY BOTHER TO DO PROJECTS LIKE THIS ONE?

William Griswold

National Park Service, Northeast
Archeology Group

FEDERAL POLICY REQUIREMENTS

Thomas King in his book *Cultural Resource Laws & Practice: An Introductory Guide,* discusses the evolution of cultural resource preservation laws and their applicability to federal properties. For almost a century now, the Federal Government has passed laws to protect cultural resources on Federal Lands, beginning in 1906 with the passage of the Antiquities Act. Since then, Congress has enacted numerous laws to regulate the management of cultural and archeological resources. Included among the most important laws are the Archeological Resources Protection Act (ARPA), The Abandoned Shipwrecks Act, The Native American Graves Protection and Repatriation Act (NAGPRA), and The National Historical Preservation Act (NHPA), just to name a few.

The last one mentioned, The National Historical Preservation Act (NHPA) was enacted by Congress in 1966 and has been amended several times since then. This one is probably the most important act to concern us here. One of the most important parts of the act, at least for archeological purposes, is Section 106. To paraphrase King and the act, Section 106 requires federal agencies to take into account the effects of their actions on any district, site, building, structure or object that is either in or that is eligible for entry in the National Register. The section also accords the Advisory Council a reasonable opportunity to comment on the undertaking.

The wording of Section 106 is designed to include anything that is either in the National Register *or eligible* for the National Register. Properties qualify for the National Register or become eligible for the National Register if it is associated with a specific important historical event(s) (Criteria A), or with a specific important historical person or persons (Criteria B). A property can also qualify if it is characteristic of a particular type of construction (Criteria C) or if it contains significant research potential (Criteria D). In other words most NPS sites qualify.

In order to "assess the effects of their actions" the NPS units work with various specialists who are set up as advisors to the parks. These specialists include archeologists, landscape architects, historic architects, collection curators, historians, and ethnologists who aid the park in evaluating their proposed actions. External organizations also aid the parks in evaluating various projects. The three most important external agencies are the State Historic Preservation Officer (SHPO), the Tribal Historic Preservation Officer (THPO), and the Advisory Council on Historic Preservation (ACHP). This review process, while at times seemingly cumbersome, protects cultural resources from ill-conceived activities. The process is not designed to completely protect archeological or cultural resources from all damages, or to deter all proposed construction plans. It simply forces mangers to think about what effect their actions may have on the resources that they are charged to care for.

To get back to the question at hand, why bother to do projects like this one? One answer is simple, the more information that we have about a park the better we can design projects and the better we can protect those valuable cultural resources. In most cases it also saves money in the long run. Almost without exception it is easier to redesign a project in its conceptual stage to minimize ground disturbance or avoid a known archeological resource than it is to mitigate the effects on an archeological site or resource during construction.

CULTURAL RESOURCE STEWARDSHIP

Another way to answer the question of why bother to do projects like this one, compels a discussion about stewardship. Stewardship, as commonly defined, denotes care and protection of something without actually owning it. None of the units within the NPS are "individually owned or operated" to borrow a phrase from the franchising establishments. These units have been chosen by Congress to have some merit to the American people as a whole. The units within the NPS are then owned collectively by the American people. The NPS is simply the federal organization established to manage and care for them.

Many of the people involved in the NPS, and especially those charged with managing cultural resources really do consider themselves as stewards. We are simply trying to manage, care for, and protect the resources within our charge for people to enjoy now, and in the future. Most of us take our job very seriously and try to represent the non-renewable cultural and

archeological resources that, without us, would not have a voice.

NPS-28, the guidelines developed for management of cultural resources within the National Park Service, defines the obligation of cultural resource managers.

> The National Park Service is steward of many of America's most important cultural, natural, and recreational resources. It is charged to preserve them unimpaired for the enjoyment of present and future generations. All park management activities stem from these resources. If they are degraded or lost, so is the essence of the park.

> Almost every park in the national park system has cultural resources, just as nearly all parks have flora and fauna. Unlike healthy ecosystems, though, the material evidence of past human activities is finite and nonrenewable. Such tangible resources begin to deteriorate almost from the moment of their creation. Once lost they cannot be recovered. In keeping with the NPS organic act of 1916 and varied historic preservation laws, park management activities must reflect awareness of the irreplaceable nature of these material resources.

Archeologists, and cultural resource managers alike, realize that National Park Service sites are for the enjoyment of everyone. One of the reasons that people travel to NPS sites is to learn about a place, and part of the NPS's mission is to educate the public about the place. The NPS employs hundreds of interpreters, historians, archeologists, ethnologists, curators, exhibit design specialists, etc. who attempt to bring the public the most accurate information about a site. However, the information that we were communicating to the public about the archeological resources at a site, was often biased toward a few areas of the park that had been investigated or toward the information derived from compliance projects. To truly understand the archeology of a site, one needs to look at the site as a whole. So then if we ask the question again, why bother to do projects like this one? The answer is to fulfill part of our mission and provide the public with the best and most accurate information about a site.

Whew, I'm glad the archeology is all done for this site!

Actually it's not. Archeology attempts to tell a story about mankind. It does so with fragmentary information. The information is fragmentary because not everything makes it into the archeological record and many things that do enter the archeological record never make it out. Think of the archeology of Liberty Island as a 1,000-piece puzzle. The work that we have done over the last three years has allowed us to put maybe 50 pieces of the puzzle together. We can begin to visualize an image of the picture depicted by the puzzle, but the picture is still vague and undefined. Most of these pieces that have been placed are scattered across the puzzle, so that it is difficult to tell what the picture is showing. It is only by putting together more pieces of the puzzle that we begin to understand the archeology of the site. As new pieces of the puzzle are added, theories, beliefs, and history of the island will be transformed.

Additional archeological work is needed to continue to reveal the image in the puzzle. For example, in this book I have not even mentioned the underwater archeological resources of the island. These resources are undoubtedly present, and when money becomes available for a proper assessment, the information will greatly add to our knowledge about the island. In a similar vein, the geophysical study concentrated on the deposits within approximately 2.5 meters of the surface of the island. Undoubtedly, there are archeological remains on the island that are buried below 2.5 meters. Borings, done with a drilling rig, additional geophysical studies, or deep trenching may illuminate the deposits below 2.5 meters. In addition to these studies, continued archeological investigations done in compliance with Section 106 of the National Historic Preservation Act will also bring to light additional information about the former uses of the island. In summary, I see the research presented in this book as a starting point for continued research on Liberty Island rather than an ending for the previous research. Much work remains to be done on the island.

Sources and Further Reading

Thomas F. King's book, *Cultural Resource Laws & Practice: An Introductory Guide* (AltaMira, Walnut Creek, CA et.al., 1998) provides an excellent discussion of the laws protecting cultural resources within the United States. Another book by King titled Federal Planning and Historic Places: the Section 106 Process (AltaMira, Walnut Creek, CA et. al. 2000) provides additional information concerning federal planning and the laws which govern it.

Several manuals and volumes have been produced for internal National Park Service use which discus how we approach cultural resources. The most important is *NPS-28, Cultural Resources Management Guideline, Release Number 4*. U.S. Department of the Interior, National Park

Service, Washington, D.C. This manual was written to promote uniform guidelines to cultural resources across the service.

GLOSSARY OF TERMS

Anatomical pertaining to the structure of plants or animals

Archaic Period the time period from approximately 10,000 – 3,000 BP marked by a hunting gathering adaptation, but without the use of ceramics.

Archeological Overview and Assessment (OA) is a document produced in the NPS which summarizes the archeological information currently available about a site, critiques excavations that have taken place in the past, and provides direction for research to be conducted at the site in the future

Archeology/Archaeology – The study of mankind through the examination of material remains, usually recovered through excavation.

Artifacts refers to any object that has been modified for use by humans.

Artillery refers to either the guns or cannons that fire projectiles or the troops who use them.

Bioturbation natural agents like roots, worms, and bugs that move things around in the soil.

BP Before Present; term used most often with Radiocarbon dates or sequences established through Radiocarbon dating and actually refers to a mid-twentieth century date corresponding to a time before nuclear testing began.

Carbon 14 dating method of dating developed by Willard Libey in the late 1940s which dates certain categories of material by assessing the amount of radioactive carbon left and comparing it to known decay rates.

Compliance a shortened form of archeological excavations conducted to fulfill requirements for Section 106 of the National Historic Preservation Act.

Contact Period refers to the time when contact occurred between Europeans and Native American groups; can vary in time from place to place, but occurs in the area around Liberty Island at the beginning of the seventeenth-century.

Counterscarp refers to the side/slope of a fortification ditch furthest away from the actual fortification; opposite the scarp or side/slope of a fortification ditch nearest the fortification.

Cultural Resource Preservation Program (CRPP) refers to a program within the NPS that provides money for various cultural resource projects; projects are evaluated by committee on an annual or semi-annual basis and projects are competitively selected.

Ecofacts are things connected with the environment that have been used by humans but have not been modified from their natural state i.e. seeds, bones, etc.

Electromagnetic Induction (EM) a method of geophysical investigation in which the variations are noted on an electromagnetic current introduced into the ground; patterning of the variation reflects burial of metallic including non-ferrous objects.

Electronic Total Station surveying instrument where everything is electronically calculated from by use of a laser.

Fauna as used in this book, refers to animal bones.

Feature is something created by man which for one reason or another cannot be taken back to the lab i.e. a pit, a building foundation, a midden, etc.

Flora plants or parts of plants

Flotation a process in which water is used to separate small artifacts and ecofacts from the soil for later analysis.

Genus/Species terms refers to the classification of living things into a family and sub-family

Geophysical Survey non-invasive equipment used to locate buried artifacts or features

GIS Geographical Information System or GIS are computer programs which allow an individual to view and manage information geographically; ArcView, the GIS program widely used in the NPS allows users to view maps and databases in different layers to look for geographical patterns

Glacis a sloping approach leading to the counterscarp

Ground Penetrating Radar (GPR) a method of geophysical investigation in which a radar signal is introduced into the ground and a profile of the ground can be viewed; different antennae frequencies allow the profile of the ground to be examined at different depths; this method is arguably the most accurate of the geophysical methods.

Hearth a feature where burning or cooking has occurred.

Infantry the foot soldiers of the army

Lithic stone modified by man; may refer to a tool or a by-product of tool production

Magazine a room where munitions are kept

Magnetometer geophysical testing instrument that detects the presence of ferrous objects or items that contain ferrous components.

Microscopy refers to microscopic examination of materials.

Midden refuse disposal heap or area.

National Register an organization that maintains a list of important historical places and evaluates new places for listing.

Paleoecology / Paleoenvironment the study of ancient environments

Paleoethnobotany the study of plants used by man that survive in the archeological record.

Paleo-Indian Period refers to the earliest period of human habitation in the New World characterized by fluted projectile points.

Parenchymatous Tissue Analysis a relatively new technique for paleoethnobotanists that involves the identification of plants through the examination of the soft tissues that are left behind.

Pest House is an old term referring to a structure, or in this case a structure and an island, used to quarantine individuals.

Photomicrographs refers to photographs made from the microscopes.

Pollen Analysis is a technique used to investigate the paleoenvironment through an analysis of the relative frequencies of various types of pollen grains.

Prehistory simply means before history, which in our case means before the arrival of the Europeans to North America.

Sallyport a gateway into the fort.

Scanning Electron Microscope (SEM) a type of microscope that permits examination of materials at the molecular level.

Scarp the side of a ditch, usually sloping, closest to the main fortifications; see opposite counterscarp

Section 106 of the National Historical Preservation Act is the section requiring managers to assess the impacts of various projects on the resources either in or eligible for inclusion in the National Register.

Shell Midden – a trash heap made of shells or shell fragments that are the physical remains of food collection activities.

Site Identification Study can be one of several different types of projects, but is one that is designed to gather information about a site or a suspected site through archeological fieldwork.

Systematic Archeological Inventory Program (SAIP) a NPS program designed for the long-term systematic collection of archeological information about a site or park.

Taphonomic Process refers to processes that happen to archeological materials and sites after they have been buried; numerous changes happen to materials once they have entered the archeological record.

Woodland Period is the latest Prehistoric Period dating from about 3,000-400 B.P. and is marked by the introduction of ceramics. Numerous other changes happen during this time period including the development of agriculture in some areas of the Northeast.

WPA Work Projects Administration was an organization developed during the great depression of the 1930 to conduct and develop public works projects.